One Arrow, One Life

Zen,

Archery,

Enlightenment

Kenneth Kushner

Illustrated by Jackson Morisawa

TUTTLE PUBLISHING
Boston • Rutland, Vermont • Tokyo

Entrance to the Kyudo dojo at Chozen-Ji

Kenneth Kushner was born in Chicago in 1949. He received a BA from the University of Wisconsin in 1971 and his PhD in clinical psychology from the University of Michigan in 1977. He began Zen training under Tanouye Tenshin Roshi in 1978, and in 1981 traveled to Hawaii and Japan to study kyudo. He currently lives in Madison, Wisconsin, where he teaches at the University of Wisconsin. He is also on the educational staff of the Institute of Zen Studies in Honolulu.

First Tuttle edition in 2000, an imprint of Periplus Editions (HK) Ltd,
with editorial offices at 153 Milk Street, Boston, Massachusetts 02109.

Library of Congress Catalog Card Number: Cataloging in Progress
ISBN: 0-8048-3246-3

Distributed by

NORTH AMERICA
Tuttle Publishing
Distribution Center
Airport Industrial Park
364 Innovation Drive
North Clarendon, VT
05759-9436
Tel: (802) 773-8930
Tel: (800) 526-2778
Fax: (802) 773-6993

JAPAN
Tuttle Publishing
RK Building, 2nd Floor
2-13-10 Shimo-Meguro,
Meguro-Ku
Tokyo 153 0064
Tel: (03) 5437-0171
Fax: (03) 5437-0755

ASIA PACIFIC
Berkeley Books Pte Ltd
5 Little Road #08-01
Singapore 536983
Tel: (65) 280-1330
Fax: (65) 280-6290

1 3 5 7 9 10 8 6 4 2
06 05 04 03 02 01 00

Printed in United States of America
Cover design by Graciela Galup

CONTENTS

ACKNOWLEDGMENTS

I would like to express my deepest gratitude to:

Tanouye Tenshin Roshi, Jackson Morisawa, and Suhara Koun Osho, who have worked patiently to make Zen and the Ways accessible to Westerners. Chozen-Ji Kyudo was created by, and reflects, their kiai. In addition, Jackson Morisawa's knowledge of kyudo, the Japanese language, and his artistic skills have contributed greatly to this book.

Two old friends and training partners, Mike Sayama and Gordon Greene, who have helped me in many ways over the years, and have also contributed much to this book; and Steve Wallman, a new friend and training partner, who has given me valuable editorial assistance.

My wife, Erica, who has accompanied me half way around the world and has tolerated long absences so that I could pursue my training.

INTRODUCTION
Entering the Way

> At first glance it must seem intolerably degrading for
> Zen—however the reader may understand this word—to
> be associated with anything so mundane as archery.
>
> Eugen Herrigel[1]

I arrived in Honolulu late in the afternoon. It was August of
1980 and I was 31 years old. I had been planning the trip for a
year and a half. Leaving my wife behind, I had recently
resigned from my job on the mainland. I had come to Hawaii
to study kyudo, the Zen Art of Archery. My destination was
Chozen-Ji, a Zen temple located in the Kalihi valley, a ten-
minute drive from downtown Honolulu.

I had written ahead to inform Tanouye Roshi[2], the abbot of
Chozen-Ji, of the time of my arrival. Usually when students
from the mainland come to Hawaii, he makes arrangements to
have them met at the airport and brought back to the temple.
However, I had explained in my letter that I would be happy to
take a cab if it would be more convenient.

After collecting my suitcase in the baggage claim area, I
looked around to see if anyone had been sent for me.
Unfortunately, I did not know who I should be looking for.
Perhaps the person from Chozen-Ji would not be able to
recognize me. I started to feel ill at ease. How long should I
wait before taking a cab? What if I took one and missed the
person who had come to meet me? My anxiety about entering a
Zen temple grew. What did this mean? Was this a message of
some sort? Zen masters are known to treat their students

1

harshly. Was this part of my training; or was it a sign I was not welcome?

Finally, after about two hours, I hailed a taxi. I gave the driver the address and was relieved when he told me that he had heard of the street the temple is on. He took the highway towards downtown Honolulu, then quickly exited on to Kalihi Street, the street that Chozen-Ji is on. The road began to climb; the higher we went, the narrower it became. The setting now looked more like a tropical rain forest than a major metropolitan area. The driver told me he had never traveled this far into the valley before. We continued to climb. He slowed down, turned right into a driveway, and told me we were there.

"What kind of place is this?" he asked.

"A Zen temple," I replied.

"I've never seen it before," he said, looking intrigued. "I'd like to come back here some time and have a better look at it."

I paid the driver, got out of the cab, and looked around. It was dusk and very still. In front of me were two sets of Japanese-style buildings separated by a large hill. I walked towards the buildings on my left and saw a sign that read, "Visitors Check in at Office." Below was an arrow that was supposed to point the way to the office. Unfortunately, I could not tell which set of buildings it pointed to.

There was still no sign of activity. I decided to check the buildings on my left. I climbed several stairs and stepped on to the verandah that ran along the outside of the building. I noticed a faint smell of incense and advanced forward. Suddenly, Tanouye Roshi came running out of the doorway. "Quiet, we're doing zazen and take your shoes off!" he said (I later saw the sign at the top of the stairs that said "no shoes past this point"). He motioned me to go back to the stairs and said, "We were wondering when you were going to arrive."

"Didn't you get my letter?" I asked.

"I got the letter," he replied. "You gave us the flight number and your arrival time. You forgot to tell us what day." He slowly shook his head from side to side.

I took my shoes off on the stairs and stepped back on to the verandah. Tanouye Roshi then showed me into the kitchen. "Hurry up and change into your training clothes," he said. "Kyudo practice starts in half an hour and you might as well go. I know this is going to be hard for you."

I changed clothes and waited in the kitchen. An older Japanese man with a shaved head and wearing priest's robes walked by on the verandah. Tanouye Roshi spoke to him in Japanese and brought him towards me. "This," said Tanouye Roshi, "is Suhara Osho." I said I was pleased to meet him. Tanouye Roshi translated.

I had been looking forward to this meeting for a year and a half. Suhara Koun Osho is a Zen priest from the Engaku-Ji temple in Kamakura, Japan, and is also a kyudo master. Tanouye Roshi had met him the year before and had invited him to come to Chozen-Ji to help establish a kyudo school there. This was the end of his second visit to Chozen-Ji; he was scheduled to return to Japan in four days. I had timed my trip to meet and train with him in Hawaii. I hoped that this introduction would make it possible to study with him in Japan later in the year. In fact, I had already arranged a job in Japan so that I would be able to support myself while training with him.

Tanouye Roshi then pointed me in the direction of the kyudo dojo and told me to go there for practice. Disoriented and embarrassed by my entrance to Chozen-Ji, I walked to the kyudo dojo for my first lesson in the Zen art of archery. Over the entrance of the dojo were four Japanese characters. Later I learned that their English translation is "One arrow, one life."

Like most Westerners, until that day what I knew of kyudo came from the book *Zen in the Art of Archery* by Eugen Herrigel. Herrigel was a German philosophy professor who spent five years in Japan during the 1930s. Wanting to study Zen, he was advised by friends to take up one of the Zen arts. Because of his previous experience with pistol shooting, Herrigel chose kyudo.

I first read Herrigel's book in 1967 as a freshman at the University of Wisconsin. It was the first book that I read in college, assigned by my English composition teacher for reasons I no longer remember. In spite of its popularity, I was disdainful of the book. I had no interest in spiritual matters and was impatient with what I considered to be vague mysticism.

Five years later, as a graduate student in psychology at the University of Michigan, I started studying another Japanese art, karate. I trained hard in it for five years, and receiving a black belt became an important goal for me. Before I could achieve that goal, I obtained my doctorate at the University of Michigan in 1977 and moved to Toledo, Ohio. I continued to prepare for my black belt examination there.

The year before I moved to Toledo, I met Mike Sayama, a fellow graduate student. I learned that he had studied martial arts at a Zen temple named Chozen-Ji in Hawaii. He invited me to practice zazen with him. Still having no interest in Zen and finding unappealing the thought of sitting cross-legged on the floor for long periods of time, I declined his invitation.

Shortly after moving to Toledo, I saw Mike demonstrate a kendo form as practiced at Chozen-Ji. I had never seen such intense concentration before in the martial arts. This was a dimension to the martial arts that was new to me. When he again invited me to train with him, I accepted.

Mike started a small training group for people interested in Zen and the martial arts. I commuted 200 miles a week to participate. Although I joined for the martial arts training, zazen was required of all participants and, reluctantly, I did zazen with them. Through the group, I became interested in Zen for the first time. Ten years after dismissing it as vague mysticism I reread *Zen in the Art of Archery* and saw it in an entirely new light.

In Zen they say that when you are ready for a teacher, the teacher finds you. In 1977, I was ready. In retrospect I was experiencing a life crisis. For as long as I could remember, my energies were focused on establishing myself professionally.

Through four years of college and six years of graduate school, I imagined that when I received my degree my life would fall into place and that I would have no worries. In 1977 I had obtained my PhD, got a good job and began to have articles accepted by professional journals. Yet, for some reason, the fulfillment that I anticipated did not accompany these successes. I was left with a growing sense of uneasiness, a feeling that there must be more to life than professional prestige. For the first time, Zen interested me. I saw Zen training as a way to find the fulfillment that was lacking in my life. Zen became the way out of my existential dilemma.

As I trained in Zen, my attitude towards the martial arts changed. Where once I saw the martial arts as means of self-defense or physical conditioning, I now saw they also afford the opportunity for spiritual growth. Soon, pursuing a black belt became yet another meaningless goal in my life; progress in the search for one's true self cannot be measured by a piece of colored cloth.

The Japanese affix the suffix "do" to the names of the Zen arts. "Do" is an important word in Zen. It is the Japanese translation of the Chinese word, "Tao." It has no direct equivalent in English, perhaps because there is no analogous concept in Western culture. "Do" is usually translated as "Way" and connotes path or road to spiritual awakening. The Zen arts can be referred to as "Ways" and are not limited to the martial arts: kyudo is the Way of the bow; kendo is the Way of the sword; karate-do is the Way of the empty fist; shodo is the Way of writing ("spiritual" calligraphy); and chado is the Way of tea (tea ceremony). Leggett described the Ways as:

fractional expressions of Zen in limited fields such as the fighting arts of sword or spear, literary arts like poetry or calligraphy, and household duties like serving tea, polishing or flower arrangement. These actions become Ways when practice is not done merely for the immediate result but also with a view to purifying, calming and focusing the psycho-physical apparatus, to attain to some degree of Zen realization and express it.[3]

It was my search for a Way that lead me to Tanouye Roshi and to Chozen-Ji. I was introduced to Tanouye Roshi by Mike Sayama, when the Roshi visited Chicago in 1978. Tanouye Roshi is a Japanese American who was a music teacher until he was certified as a Zen master in 1975. Chozen-Ji and its training center, the International Zen Dojo of Hawaii, were founded in 1972 by his teacher, Omori Sogen Rotaishi, who is direct dharma successor to the Tenryuji line of Rinzai Zen. This tradition emphasizes the integration of zazen with the Asian martial and fine arts. Thus, all students at Chozen-Ji practice zazen and most study a martial and/or a fine art. Tanouye Roshi himself has studied the martial arts for years, with an emphasis on judo and kendo.

Shortly before my second meeting with Tanouye Roshi in 1979 I had injured my knee and had to interrupt my training in karate. My interest in karate was waning anyway, especially as I was exposed to aikido in our training group. Hoping that he would say aikido, I asked Tanouye Roshi what would be the best martial art for me to study. I was surprised when he suggested kyudo. He gave several reasons for this recommendation. First, he thought that it would be easier on my knees than karate. Second, he said that at my age (29) I was too old to gain mastery in karate, aikido, or any of the more physically active martial arts. Finally, he thought that training in kyudo would be a good way to improve my poor posture.

I can think of few other times in my life when a decision felt so correct. In spite of the fact that I had never considered studying kyudo before, I had the sudden sense that studying it was not just the right thing to do but that it was an obvious choice. I thought back to Herrigel's book and it seemed to outline the type of spiritual path that I was looking for. Since kyudo instruction was practically unavailable on the United

States mainland, Tanouye Roshi suggested that I come to Chozen-Ji. I immediately started making arrangements to spend a prolonged period there.

Kyudo training had just started at Chozen-Ji. The previous year, Tanouye Roshi accompanied Omori Rotaishi on a cultural exchange to Europe sponsored by the Japanese government. It was on that trip he met Suhara Koun Osho, who was also participating in the cultural exchange. Tanouye Roshi invited him to come to Chozen-Ji to help Jackson Morisawa, one of Tanouye Roshi's students, establish a kyudo school there.

Upon returning from Japan in 1981, I moved to Madison, Wisconsin. I have returned to Chozen-Ji once or twice a year to continue my training with Mr. Morisawa. On my third visit to the temple, in 1983, Tanouye Roshi suggested that I write a book that would help Westerners better to understand kyudo; that is my hope in writing this book.

In spite of the immense popularity of *Zen in the Art of Archery*, one of the most widely read books on Zen ever published in the West, little is known about kyudo in the West today. While judo and karate are household words, few people would even recognize the Japanese name for the Way of the bow. No doubt this is due to the fact that Herrigel never used the word "kyudo" in his book. Kyudo instruction is still almost unavailable in the United States, in contrast to what must be thousands of schools of other martial arts. Until very recently, Americans interested in kyudo were obliged to travel to Japan for instruction.

My primary focus will be on the relationship between kyudo and Zen. In so doing, I will attempt to expand on the relationship between kyudo and traditional Zen training that was described by Herrigel. The beauty of *Zen in the Art of Archery* is its brevity and simplicity. Herrigel did not elaborate on many of the philosophical and technical points to which he alluded. My intent is to explain these to the present reader and to put them in the context of Zen training.

My understanding of Zen and kyudo has been shaped by the philosophies of my teachers. In this regard there is one fundamental way in which the philosophy of kyudo training at Chozen-Ji differs from that described by Herrigel. In the Chozen-Ji school of kyudo, the practice of kyudo is integrated with the practice of zazen. At Chozen-Ji, training in the Ways and zazen are complementary processes. Training in kyudo facilitates one's progress in zazen, and one's progress in zazen facilitates one's kyudo.

In this book, I hope to elucidate this complementarity between kyudo and zazen. What I will say about kyudo applies to any Zen art. Most people who study martial arts do not practice zazen. Conversely, most people who train in zazen do not study a Zen art. My hope is that this book will help bridge the gap between Zen training and training in all of the Ways.

This book is not intended as an instruction manual in either kyudo or zazen. The reader should not expect to learn how to practice kyudo or zazen by reading it. Rather, I hope to explain why someone would want to study kyudo; how something as "mundane" as archery can be elevated to a serious spiritual experience when it is studied as a Way. In order to view kyudo as a truly spiritual endeavor, one must treat it as a microcosm of life. In this book I will try to explain how principles involved in the seemingly simple process of shooting an arrow at a target can have profound implications for how one leads one's life.

For readers who may be interested in learning more about the Chozen-Ji traditions of kyudo in particular and of Zen training in general, there are two books that I recommend. First, for those interested in learning more about kyudo, I recommend the book *Zen Kyudo* by my teacher, Jackson Morisawa.[4] It is a comprehensive treatise on the Chozen-Ji school of kyudo. It delves into the technical, philosophical and spiritual aspects of Chozen-Ji kyudo to a far greater extent than I will in this book. It includes detailed explanations and diagrams of the techniques and procedures of kyudo. Readers

who are looking for instruction in zazen would be interested in
the book *Samadhi: Self Development in Zen, Swordsmanship,
and Psychotherapy*, by Mike Sayama,[5] which has translations
of instructions by Omori Sogen Rotaishi. Dr. Sayama's book is
also of particular interest for anyone interested in learning
more about the philosophy and lineage of Zen training at
Chozen-Ji. It also elucidates the psychological aspects of Zen
and Zen training in much greater depth than I will in this book.

CHAPTER 1
Techniques and Principles

Thousands of repetitions and out of one's true self
perfection emerges.

Zen Saying

Suhara Osho left Chozen-Ji for Japan four days after I arrived
in Hawaii. I left for Japan four months after that. I had planned
my stay in Japan so that it would be convenient to train with
Suhara Osho. My wife and I both arranged part-time teaching
jobs through the University of Maryland's Far East Division. I
had chosen Yokosuka as my teaching site in order to be close
to Suhara Osho's dojo in Kamakura. Even though my plans
were based on training with Suhara Osho, I hesitated to ask him
directly, before he left Hawaii, if I could study with him in
Japan. I thought that such a blunt question, coming from a
near stranger, would be a violation of Japanese customs.
Instead, I told him I was planning to spend some time in Japan
and that I would be working near Kamakura. He gave me his
address and invited me to stop by and see him.

I called Suhara Osho the day I arrived in Japan. Through an
interpreter I explained I had trained briefly with him in Hawaii
and that he suggested that I look him up. I had no idea if he
remembered who I was. To my dismay, he told me he was very
busy and that I should call him back in two weeks. Exactly two
weeks later I called again and was told that he was still very
busy and could not see me for one month. My disappointment
grew. My time in Japan was limited; I wondered if I would be
able to train with him at all. Exactly one month later I called
back and this time was told that he could see me later in the

week. He gave me instructions on how to get there and told me he would have somebody there to interpret.

It was a two-hour train ride from where I was living to Kamakura. I got off the train at the Kita-Kamakura station and walked up the steps towards the entrance of Engaku-Ji. It was mid-April and pouring rain. The ground was muddy and the air smelled of cherry blossoms. The gate keeper to the temple had obviously been warned that I would be coming. He took one look at me and said asked, "Suhara Osho?" I nodded and we both laughed nervously. He then proceeded to lead me to the kyudo dojo.

I entered the grounds of the dojo alone. Seeing no one, I walked over to the main building of the dojo and looked in. There was no one there. Thinking that I would go in and wait, I looked for a place to take my shoes off. I wanted to avoid a repeat of my entry into Chozen-Ji. Just then, I heard somebody yell "Hallooo." I looked around and saw Suhara Osho, dressed in black temple work clothes, waving his arms at me. I went over, bowed, and he motioned me into a little wooden building (I was to find out later that Mrs. Suhara runs a small concession selling tea to tourists on the grounds of the dojo and that this was where she prepared the tea).

After I entered, a Japanese woman appeared. She introduced herself in English as a kyudo student whom Suhara Osho had asked to help find an interpreter. She went on to explain that an interpreter would be coming soon. She excused herself and left me alone with Suhara Osho. He made two bowls of matcha, the type of tea used in tea ceremony. We set in silence as I watched him froth up the tea with a bamboo whisk. We drank in silence, unable to converse. After some time, the woman arrived with the interpreter, an American who was a friend of hers.

Suhara Osho and the woman very politely started asking me questions. First they wanted to know the nature of this visit. I said that it was to say "hello" and to see if it would be possible to train here. They asked where I was living. I said in Zama (which I had learned that day was two hours away by train). I was told that perhaps commuting from Zama would be too inconvenient. I told them that I did not mind the train ride. I was told there was a kyudo dojo in the city of Zama. I told them I would check but that I would still like to study in Kamakura.

The conversation went on in this vein for some time. In my view, they were doing their best to discourage me from training there. It is not uncommon for Japanese teachers to test prospective students by trying to discourage them. I hoped that was why Suhara Osho asked me to wait six weeks before agreeing to see me and why they now seemed so intent on my studying elsewhere. I decided to wait patiently until I got a clear acceptance or rejection.

At one point Suhara Osho left, leaving me alone with the woman and the interpreter. She continued to ask questions. She asked me about my experiences training at Chozen-Ji. She wanted to know if I had shot at the mato or only at the makiwara.

A makiwara is a practice target made out of bundled straw. It is shot at from a range of three to four feet, as opposed to the paper mato, or "real target", shot at from a distance of 28 metres (90 feet). In traditional kyudo training, students could spend years shooting at the makiwara before they were allowed to shoot at the mato. Most training described by Herrigel in *Zen in the Art of Archery* involved makiwara training. I have been told that Herrigel shot at the makiwara for four out of the five years that he spent in Japan. In contemporary Japan, makiwara training is not stressed as it once was, and students are often allowed to shoot at the mato after only a few weeks. Students, particularly Westerners, are often overly impatient to shoot at the mato.

I replied that I had shot at the mato in Hawaii. I was then told that people shoot at the makiwara for a long time at this dojo. I was given the example of a Westerner who had done so for many months. I replied that it would be fine with me.

Actually, I never expected that I would be allowed to shoot at the mato at all in Japan. While I had shot at the mato in Hawaii, makiwara training was still stressed there and I had been told this would most likely to continue if I studied with Suhara Osho. When I was told that I should expect to train only with the makiwara I was not surprised.

After the questions about the makiwara the tone of the conversation became less serious. Suhara Osho came back and told me that I was welcome to train there. I was given a tour of the dojo and my training schedule was arranged. Two days later I returned to Engaku-Ji for my first lesson with Suhara Osho. The first thing that he asked me to do was shoot at the mato. Suhara Osho suggested that I also study with Onuma Sensei at the Toshima-ku dojo in Tokyo. I was fortunate that he also accepted me as a student. He also asked me to shoot at the mato.

In retrospect it seems that the question of whether I was willing to train at the makiwara was a test of my seriousness as a student. For the contemporary kyudo student, perhaps particularly for an American, the willingness to forestall one's attraction to the mato and to concentrate on the makiwara can be an important test of whether or not he has the discipline that kyudo requires.

Written on the makiwara stand in the kyudo dojo at Chozen-Ji, in calligraphy done by Omori Sogen Rotaishi, is the Japanese phrase "Hyakuren Jitoku." Jackson Morisawa translates this saying as "Thousands of repetitions and out of one's true self perfection emerges." In explaining this saying in his book, *Zen Kyudo*, he writes:

> To make a good sword takes repeated heating, pounding, and sharpening which require tremendous discipline in a state of order and control. If one instills this kind of discipline in repetitive, innovative, and observant training in kyudo, he will be able to taste the satisfaction of his own effort within himself.[1]

The placement of this saying on the makiwara stand is most appropriate, for traditionally the makiwara has been the anvil on which the kyudo student forged his technique. Because it is shot at from point blank range, the makiwara provides a way in which the student can practice the basics of kyudo without being distracted with concerns about hitting the target. Omori Rotaishi's calligraphy gives caution not to abandon the makiwara prematurely. There is no substitute for makiwara practice, just as there is no substitute for dedicated and repetitious practice of the art itself.

Kyudo training, whether shooting at the makiwara or the mato, is a formalized procedure for shooting arrows. This procedure is called "hassetsu," which is usually translated as the eight steps or stages of kyudo. The specifics of hassetsu may differ slightly across the various schools of kyudo. While there is some variation in the movements preceding the performance of hassetsu, depending on the formality of the occasion and on the specific school of kyudo, the student practices the same eight steps over and over through the years. To the uninitiated, it may seem that the techniques of kyudo are simple, for how long can it take to master a sequence of eight steps? However, nothing could be further from the truth. The techniques of hassetsu are extremely complex. Every aspect of shooting, from the distribution of the body's weight on one's feet to the rhythm of one's breathing, is standardized. The more one practices kyudo, the more one becomes aware of the subtleties of the techniques of the eight steps. It is said that it takes a minimum of thirty years to master the grip. The eight stages of kyudo are described and illustrated in the drawings at the end of this chapter (pp.19–27).

The idea of teaching an art through standardized sets of techniques is found in all of the Ways. In kyudo, there are relatively few such techniques, and those are found in hassetsu. In this regard, kyudo is similar to tea ceremony which involves the repetitive practice of the same ritual of preparing and drinking tea. Other Zen arts, particularly the martial arts, have more techniques. Judo, aikido, and kendo, for example, all have hundreds if not thousands of techniques which must be mastered by the student. A student will spend years copying and imitating the techniques he is taught by his teacher. Modification of these techniques is not encouraged and is likely to be frowned upon by the teacher. Such uncritical acceptance and practice of standardized techniques is difficult for many Westerners, who are accustomed to questioning and modifying what they are taught to suit their own needs.

There is a Japanese word – ji – which refers to the technical aspects of a Zen art. In kyudo, ji refers to the techniques found in hassetsu, the eight stages of kyudo. However in kyudo, as in all of the Zen arts, mere mastery of ji, or techniques, is not seen as the endpoint. In order to understand this, it is necessary to consider another Japanese word that is closely related to ji. This term is ri and it has no English equivalent. Ri can best be understood as universal truths or as the underlying principles of the Universe.

Ri is formless and unchanging. Ri is ineffable; it is impossible to describe adequately underlying principles in words. Because principles have no form, the way they manifest themselves will vary from situation to situation. Specific manifestations of ri also are referred to as ji. Thus, in the Ways, techniques are seen as specific manifestations of the underlying principles. Ji is an embodiment of ri in specific situations, but is not itself ri in the same sense that a specific recipe is not in itself the underlying principles of cooking.

It is possible to gain a high level of proficiency in an art by mastering techniques. For example, one might be able to become skillful in self-defense by mastering the techniques of judo or karate-do, just as one might be able to become an accurate archer in kyudo. But this is not the intent of the Ways. Mere technical mastery is not true mastery. To rely on techniques means that one is limited to the specific techniques at which one is proficient. In this vein, Leggett writes:

The individual techniques learned in one of the arts will never fit the circumstances. Even in judo, where the techniques are very numerous, one tends to rely on certain ones which have been mastered, even if they are not absolutely appropriate. There are means of forcing the situation a little to bring off a favorite trick. This is skillful ji, but it cannot be said to be ri.[2]

True mastery comes when one understands the underlying principles of the art.

One example of ji and ri, techniques and underlying principles, in kyudo is found in the process of aiming. There are several accepted techniques of aiming. In one such technique, called the "moon at daybreak"[3] the kyudoka (practitioner of kyudo[4]) positions the bow so that the area of the bow directly on top of the grip blocks the center of the target from the kyudoka's vision. Since that part of the bow is wrapped with thin pieces of cord, it is possible to count, or estimate, the number of wraps one sees below the center of the target when one hits the target. Through trial and error the kyudoka can find a sighting point on the wrappings which is likely to produce accurate shots, just as one adjusts the cross-hairs on a rifle sight. However, to rely on this technique has certain limitations. First, the level of wrapping used for sighting will vary from bow to bow depending on the thickness of the wrappings. Second, the thrust of a bow varies with the temperature and humidity. Thus, different sighting points would have to be established in accord with different climatic factors. Similarly, the speed and the direction of the wind can also affect the arrow's trajectory and thus would also have to be taken into account. Finally, to say that one can actually establish an exact sighting point is an oversimplification of what actually happens. No kyudoka, regardless of his level of proficiency, can hold the bow and arrow perfectly still. This is more true in Japanese than in Western archery due to the mechanical differences between modern Western bows and the traditional

Japanese bow. Even with a kyudo master, at full draw one will notice that the tip of the arrow oscillates. While the range of the oscillations is slight, it is enough to mean the difference between hitting and missing the target. The kyudoka must somehow "decide" at what point in the cycle of oscillations to release the arrow. It is not possible to describe adequately how this is done, for it is done by feel, by intuition. Any technique, such as the moon at daybreak method of sighting, is only an approximation of what occurs in a proper shot. Such a technique can only bring a kyudoka to a certain point. After that, his intuition must take over. When done properly, the specific techniques of shooting are transcended as the kyudoka transcends ji and acts in accordance with ri. In the Ways, ji connotes skill and ri connotes inspiration. When one sees into the underlying principles, one's performance becomes inspired.

Understanding the principles underlying a Zen art is not based on cognitive or intellectual understanding. Rather, it is based on an intuitive awareness of the underlying principles of the Universe as they apply to that particular art. It is a form of Zen insight as it applies to that particular activity. For that reason, Leggett describes the Ways as "fractional expressions of Zen in limited fields."[5]

Because they are formless, the underlying principles of an art cannot be fully described nor directly taught. The philosophy of teaching in the Zen arts is to teach underlying principles through the repetitive practice of techniques. The techniques of the arts represent formalizations of the masters' understandings of the principles. They can be seen as approximations of the underlying principles. Thus, hassetsu is a set of techniques that are at best approximations of the naturally correct way to shoot an arrow. These techniques can only bring the student to a certain point. Each student ultimately must see into those underlying principles by himself. This can only be done by endless repetition of the eight stages of kyudo. This leads to a deeper explanation of the saying "thousands of repetitions and out of one's true self perfection emerges." In kyudo, as in the other Ways, Zen understanding—discovery of one's true self—comes only through disciplined, repetitious practice.

HASSETSU
(The Eight Stages of Kyudo)

STAGE I   *Ashibumi* (To step or tread) While standing at a right angle
to the target, the kyudoka points his left foot towards the target, then
slides his right foot in the opposite direction. On completion, the feet
are approximately one and one half shoulder's width apart and form a
60-degree angle. The stance directly sets up the next stage, *Dozukuri*.

STAGE II *Dozukuri*
(Setting the torso) The
muscles of the buttocks and
inner legs are tightened,
thrusting the lower
abdomen forward. This
places the *tanden* (energy
center below the navel)
over the base created by the
feet, stabilizing the stance.

STAGE III *Yugamae* (Setting the bow) The grip of the gloved right hand on the string and arrow and the grip of the left hand on the bow are properly established. The kyudoka turns his head towards the target and views the target area. He then returns his head to the original position (so he is looking straight ahead). Prior to lifting the bow, he turns his head once again towards the target.

STAGE IV *Uchiokoshi*
(Lifting the bow) Keeping the
arrow parallel to the ground at
all times, the bow is slowly
raised until the arrow is above
the head, and the arms are
elevated at 45-degree angles.

STAGE V   *Hikiwake* (To draw apart) The first part of this stage is known as *Daisan*, the "great third," because the bow is drawn apart one third. The kyudoka pushes his left hand towards the target. The right hand naturally follows the movement of the left and the right elbow bends at a right angle.

STAGE V *Hikiwake*
(continued) (To draw
apart) After a slight pause
at daisan, the draw
continues. Still keeping the
arrow parallel to the base,
the left hand is pushed
toward the target while the
right elbow is pulled away
from it with equal force. At
completion, the arrow is
touching the cheek, in line
with the mouth.

STAGE VI *Kai* (The meeting)
The completed form of
hikiwake is maintained.
Although the arrow is fully
drawn, the downward pressure
of the breath and the
simultaneous lifting of the nape
of the neck causes the chest to
expand, which steadily increases
the drawing tension on the bow.
The kyudoka seeks to create his
spiritual center by aligning the
horizontal and vertical forces of
the draw so they meet at right
angles in a "perfect cross."

STAGE VII *Hanare* (To release) When
the alignments of kai are completed, the
tension grows until the string slips away
from the gloved hand and the arrow looses
itself towards the target. The sudden
release of accumulated tension causes the
right hand to be thrust backwards in a
straight line, pivoting on the elbow; the
bow arm is thrust forward and to the left
as the chest attains maximal expansion.

STAGE VIII *Zanshin* (Remaining
heart or mind) The outward and
parallel propulsion of the arms at
hanare create the form of a cross with
the body. This position is held for the
duration of a brief and uninterrupted
inhalation; then the bow is lowered.
The balance of breath, posture, and
concentration, established in the
shooting sequence, continues. The
kyudoka maintains an alert mind and
remains calm and composed.

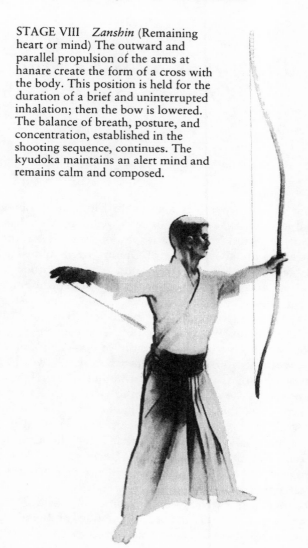

CHAPTER 2
Breathing, Posture, and Concentration

Zen without realization of the body is empty speculation.

Omori Sogen Rotaishi

During my first week at Chozen-Ji, Tanouye Roshi gave a special lecture to the four of us who were live-in students. The topic of the lecture was the principles of zazen. It was then that I first heard the above quote of Omori Sogen Rotaishi. It is a fundamental reality of Zen and a corner stone of the philosophy of training at Chozen-Ji. The statement emphasizes that Zen is not just a philosophy or an intellectual system; Zen realization is physical as well as mental. This is a difficult concept for many Westerners, especially those exposed to Zen by books only. In fact, it is common for books on Zen to begin with caveats about overemphasizing the value of words. Unlike some of the other sects of Buddhism and other religions, Zen does not stress the study of written scriptures. Direct experience and action are the important things to the Zen student. The Zen student is not asked to accept to doctrine on faith. Rather, he is asked to train so that he might have personal experience of the Oneness of the Universe. The key to this experience is the discipline known as zazen. Zen training has no real significance without it.

The process of zazen has been traditionally divided into three aspects: regulation of posture, regulation of breathing, and regulation of mental activity (concentration). Actually this division is only a convenience for the sake of explanation. In practice zazen is the unification of breathing, posture and concentration. Each aspect affects and is affected by the other two. In the Ways, one finds these principles of breathing, posture, and concentration applied to specific activities.

I will now discuss in turn the three component processes of breathing, posture and concentration.

BREATHING

The importance of proper breathing in Zen cannot be overstated, yet the concept that breathing can be a key to spirituality is still a foreign one to most Westerners. While Western people may accept the importance of breathing in athletic endeavors or in relaxation exercises, they do not generally see breath control as a prerequisite for a spiritual experience.

The major differences between breathing in Zen and what most people would consider "normal" breathing is that in Zen it is much slower and is controlled by the muscles of the lower abdomen, not those of the chest. The average person breathes at a rate of approximately 18 respirations per minute. Zen masters have been found to breathe at a rate of 4 respirations per minute or less during zazen.

In order to understand the nature of abdominal breathing in zazen, it would be helpful for me introduce two important Japanese terms that are generally unknown to Westerners. The first is hara. Physically, hara refers to the entire lower abdomen, the part below the navel. The second term is the tanden, which is the point approximately one and one half inches below the naval and is the center of the hara. In the Zen tradition, the tanden is seen to be the center of the person, both physically and psychologically. Physically, it is the person's center of gravity. Psychologically, it is seen as the center of the personality.

To say that breathing in Zen is abdominal is to say that it is controlled by the muscles of the hara. Inhalation is accomplished by relaxing the muscles of the hara. This automatically relaxes the diaphragm and air is effortlessly brought into the lungs, just as relaxing the bulb of a medicine dropper draws water up the pipette. The result is that the lower abdomen protrudes. Once the lungs are full, the person bears down on the muscles of the hara and begins the exhalation. This initial bearing down at the beginning of an exhalation is referred to as "setting" the hara. The exhalation lasts considerably longer than the inhalation. The feeling is that the air is being forced directly downward into the hara. Actually, the tensing of the hara muscles contracts the diaphragm, forcing the air out of the lungs. The muscles are contracted in such a way that the hara remains protruded and the area immediately above the naval becomes concave, with the naval pointing up. The lower abdomen remains protruded throughout both inhalation and exhalation; hence the origin of the term "Buddha belly." After continual practice, the contour of the Zen student changes. His lower abdomen remains slightly protruded and the area above it remains concave even when he is not sitting zazen. In zazen, the student constantly monitors his breathing. When he notices that the quality of his breathing has deteriorated, he adjusts it so that it is correct.

Hara is a word that has no equivalent in English. Not only does it literally refer to the geographical area of the body roughly described as the lower abdomen but it also is a word replete with psychological and spiritual connotations. To say that someone has "hara" conveys the sense that he is balanced, secure both physically and psychologically.[1] From a physical standpoint, the person with hara has a lower center of gravity than does the person with the traditional Western postural ideal of "stomach in and chest out." It is literally more difficult to tip over a person with hara, a principle that is very important in all of the martial arts and in Japanese Sumo wrestling. The person with typical Western posture is top heavy due to muscular tension in the upper body, and thus is less balanced.

To say that someone has hara also conveys the sense that he

is in balance emotionally. He does not fly off the handle, he can take in his stride whatever problems come his way. In Japanese, to say that one's hara rose or that one "lost his hara" means that he has lost his temper.

To say that one has hara also implies a sense of courage, the ability to face adversity with poise and dignity. In this regard, Von Durckheim related the following account of an event that took place during World War II:

> When the leader of the Japanese Women's Associations, on her return from a visit to Germany, spoke in a lecture of the impressive air-raid precautions she'd seen there, she added "we have nothing of all that but we have something else, we have Hara". The interpreter was greatly embarrassed. How should he translate that? What could he do but simply say "belly"? Silence, laughter. Only a few Westerners understood what was meant, but the Japanese knew that the lecturer had quite simply meant that power which, even if it gave no protection against annihilation by bombs, yet made possible an inner calm from which springs the greatest possible capacity for endurance.[2]

Hara also conveys a sense of generosity. While in English we would say that someone has a big heart, in Japan they would say that he has a big hara. Hara also implies strength. To do something with hara means to do something with all your might, to give it your best. The person with hara is seen as being physically stronger and stronger of character.

The connections between the physical and psychological aspects of hara are not just metaphorical to the Zen student. With training, he comes to understand that his psychological state fluctuates with the quality of his breathing. He learns that when he is carried away by anger or when he is overcome by fear or anxiety, his breathing becomes fast and shallow. He loses the pressure in his lower abdomen and his center of gravity rises towards his shoulders. He becomes physically less stable. He also learns to control his emotional reactions by controlling his breathing. Through proper breathing in the middle of adversity, he can maintain his psychological equillibrium.

Several years after beginning my Zen training, I testified for the first time as an expert psychological witness. From the start I was quite anxious, particularly when I discovered how hostile the opposing attorney was. On the witness stand, I noticed that whenever I felt nervous, my breathing became quicker and more shallow and that I was using my chest muscles rather than my lower abdomen. After making this connection, I deliberately set my hara, slowed my rate of breathing, and calmed myself. For two hours on the witness stand I set my hara whenever I noticed my breath rising. While I had to do it frequently, I feel that it greatly helped my performance in court. This was the first time that I was able to control my anxiety in a tense situation by applying the principles of zazen breathing.

Hara breathing is the natural way to breathe. Babies breathe abdominally and have noticeable haras. However, as the child grows, he develops the habit of breathing from the chest and acquires chronic muscular tension in his upper torso. In Zen training, one strives to reverse the habit of thoracic breathing.

Beginning Zen students are often frustrated by their inability to breathe properly. This was certainly the case for me. Try as I might, I could not get my lower abdomen to relax on inhalation. On exhalation I would try to force air downwards towards my tanden. Yet my breathing remained shallow and my chest, rather than my lower abdomen, moved. I even came to believe the concept of hara was a hoax. Then, one day, I was explaining to a friend that I was angry at another person. As I related the circumstances, I found myself reliving the anger. Suddenly I noticed I was breathing differently. For the first time I could relax my lower abdominal muscles. Finally I could feel my hara. This experience is sometimes referred to as having one's stomach "drop." The training necessary first to experience one's hara will vary from person to person. For some people it is an instantaneous event, as it was in my case. For others it appears to be a more gradual process. In every case, as one trains, one's breathing becomes deeper and deeper and one's stomach continues to drop.

The manner of breathing in kyudo is identical to that in zazen. Inhalations are begun by relaxing the lower abdominal muscles. On exhalation the kyudoka forces his breath into his hara, making it protrude. A rhythm of slow, deep breathing is established in the sequence of shooting and every movement is coordinated with this rhythm. It is prescribed whether each move is done on an inhalation or an exhalation. Those requiring the most power, such as drawing the bow and holding it at full draw, are done on exhalations. The power of those motions come from the breath. As in zazen, the kyudoka continually adjusts his breathing to keep it in proper rhythm and from his hara.

An important example of the power of breath in kyudo is the release of the arrow. As the kyudoka holds the arrow at full draw, he bears down on his hara with his breath. This pressure expands the chest and shoulders. The expansion thrusts the left hand, which holds the bow, towards the target. Simultaneously, it propels the right elbow in the opposite direction, away from the target. Throughout the stage of kai, the arrow continues to be subtly drawn by the opposing motions of the right and left arms. Eventually the tension allows the string to slip from the kyudoka's gloved right hand, releasing the arrow.

It is possible, although incorrect, to release the arrow without the power of one's breath. This can be done by simply letting go of the string with the right hand, as one would in Western archery. In this case, the arrow will not travel far. Or, the kyudoka can use the muscles of wrists and arms to push the left hand towards the target while pulling the string with the right hand. This release is more sophisticated than merely letting go of the string and it is possible to shoot the arrow far enough to hit the mato. Finally, the kyudoka can simply contract his shoulder muscles and create tension that will release the arrow. This, too, will result in an even more powerful shot.

All of the above examples of incorrect shots would be obvious to an observer sophisticated in kyudo because the tension is in the upper body and not in the hara. The kyudoka would look top heavy, his center of gravity located in his chest. When done properly, the lower abdomen protrudes and muscles of the arms and shoulders are relaxed. The center of gravity is then in the tanden.

My understanding of the release has changed with improvements in my breathing. When I trained during my first stay in Hawaii, I usually released the arrow by merely letting go of the string. When I started studying in Japan, I grasped the idea that tension caused by the opposing motions of the right and left sides releases the arrow. However, I began using my wrist muscles to create the tension. By turning both wrists away from the target, I was able to add power to the release.

I was continually corrected on my release. My instructor told me to use my hara, not my wrists. The best I could do, however, was to generate tension by thrusting my left arm towards the target and pulling my right elbow away from the target. This resulted in a more powerful release. My breathing also felt better, my center of gravity lower. Again, I was corrected: I was still relying too much on the muscles of my arms and my breathing was still too shallow.

As my training continued, the focal point of my release has come closer to my tanden. From tension in my forearms, it progressed to tension in my upper arms, next to tension in my shoulder blades. Each progression was accompanied by a lowering of my breath and increased use of my hara in the release. I understand that this progression continues throughout one's training; eventually the focal point of the release becomes the tanden.

The steps of shooting an arrow are preceded by preliminary movements. This includes bowing before the target, stepping towards the shooting mark, and nocking the arrow on the string. Depending on the formality of the occasion, one might kneel before the target and bow. In a sharei, or ceremonial shooting, these preliminary movements involve a number of steps, kneelings, and bows and can take as much as five minutes. Regardless of the degree of formality, all of these preliminary motions are done slowly, deliberately, and in rhythm with one's breath. In this way, one establishes proper breathing before the process of shooting actually begins. Similar motions follow the completion of the shot and, again, proper breathing is maintained throughout.

POSTURE

Proper posture facilitates proper breathing. The postures traditionally assumed in zazen, the lotus and half lotus positions, greatly facilitate abdominal breathing. Figure 1 shows a person performing zazen in the lotus position. There

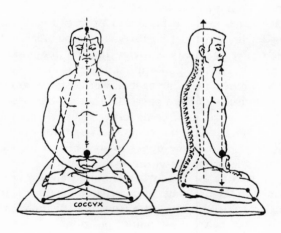

COCCYX

Figure 1   Zazen posture

are several important aspects to posture. First, the body is firmly and securely seated and the body's weight is evenly distributed on the ground. The stability is due to a triangle formed by the knees and coccyx (tail bone). The triangle keeps the body in balance and gives it a firm base against which the person can bear down with his breath when he exhales.

The second important feature of proper zazen posture is the person's hips. They are thrust forward so that the tanden is centered roughly in the middle of the imaginary triangle formed by the knees and coccyx. In this position the hara is unrestricted and the abdominal muscles are more easily relaxed.

The third aspect of posture is the position of the spine. It is in its natural position with slight curves in the lower and upper back, while the neck is straight. In this natural position, the bones of the spine support the upper torso and the chest, back, shoulder and neck muscles are free to relax. Once relaxed the chest muscles are no longer needed for breathing, allowing the muscles of the hara to take over.

Just as proper posture facilitates proper breathing, proper breathing facilitates proper posture. When one breathes from the hara, the center of gravity is lower. In turn, the upper torso is balanced and, like a child's inflatable punching bag clown, rights itself immediately due to its lower center of gravity. As a result, the muscles of the upper torso, otherwise used to keep the body in balance, are free to relax. The body is more stable and it is easier to keep the spine in its natural position. This makes it easy to relax the upper torso while at the same time maintaining the proper position of the spine.

The posture one assumes when shooting an arrow in kyudo is illustrated in the drawings of hassetsu in Chapter 1 and again in Figure 2. It is essentially a transposition of the principles of posture in zazen to a standing position. A firm base is established by spreading the feet about one and one half shoulder's width. The feet are turned outwards, so that the angle between the big toes is approximately 60 degrees. The

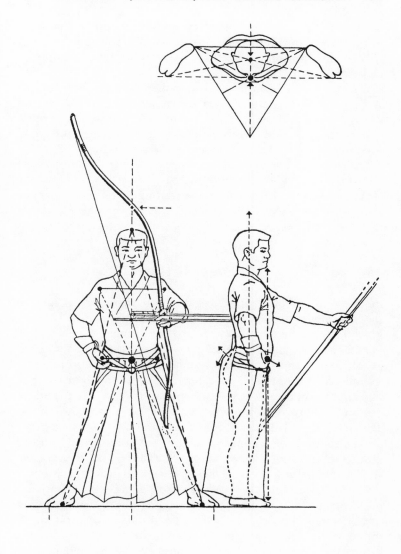

Figure 2   Kuydo stage (stance of dozukuri)

pelvis is thrust forward, extending the tanden and putting force in the hara. The spine maintains its natural position. This is a very stable position and, like the basic zazen posture, it facilitates proper breathing.

Breathing and posture work together in the release of the arrow. As the kyudoka bears down with his breath at full draw, he extends the nape of his neck upward. This motion allows the force of his breath to straighten his spine and expand his chest, thereby powering the release.

Proper posture is maintained throughout the motions before and after the eight stages of shooting an arrow. When one moves, kneels, and bows in the ceremony before and after the shot, a secure, balanced base is maintained; the pelvis is thrust forward, and the spine remains in its natural position.

CONCENTRATION

In the Rinzai sect of Zen, beginning students are taught to regulate their concentration with a technique called called susoku which, in Japanese, means "counting the breath." In the Chozen-Ji tradition the student is instructed to count each exhalation. When he reaches ten, he is to go back to one and resumes counting. If he loses count, he resumes with one. While this might sound easy, it is extremely difficult. Many beginners are quite surprised at how poor their concentration is. Thoughts of all kinds arise to distract the student from concentrating on counting the breath. By continually bringing his attention back to the basic task of counting the breaths, the student learns to keep from being distracted from the count.

Through susoku, the student also learns that breathing, posture, and concentration are interconnected. When breathing and posture are good, it is easier to maintain concentration on the count. If breathing or posture should lapse, concentration is lost. Should one's concentration lapse, breathing and posture also deteriorate. Thus, one maintains one's concentration by constant regulation of breathing and posture just as concentrating on counting one's breath forces one to maintain good posture and breathing.

In the Rinzai sect, after a beginning student has practiced susoku for a period of time, he is given a second type of concentration exercise called a koan. A koan is a question, given to the student by a Zen master, which cannot be answered by one's rational mind. "What is the sound of one hand clapping?" is an example of a koan widely known in the West. Once given a koan, answering it becomes the focus of one's concentration during zazen.

For the student of kyudo, the process of kyudo itself is an exercise in concentration. At all times, he tries to pay full attention to what he is doing. From the preliminary bow, to the release of the arrow, to the final bow, he strives to concentrate fully, without interruption. Just as in susoku, when the student notices his concentration has lapsed, he adjusts his breathing and posture and focuses again on the task at hand. Thus, the same interplay between breathing, posture, and concentration found in zazen applies to kyudo.

Earlier I explained that Zen discipline results in physical changes: the abdomen protrudes, the upper torso relaxes, the center of gravity lowers. Zen discipline also results in mental changes. The student finds that his concentration improves; he is able to remain free from distracting thoughts for longer periods of time. Eventually he experiences a new state of mind and he will enter the realm of Zen awareness.

Suhara Koun Osho performing sharei at Wisconsin State Historical
Society Museum (photo courtesy of Carolyn Pflasterer)

CHAPTER 3
Mushin

"One arrow, one life."

Kyudo Saying

In July of 1983, I participated in a kyudo demonstration with Suhara Osho and Jackson Morisawa at the Wisconsin State Historical Society Museum. I had organized the demonstration and was anxious about how it would be received. I was very pleased when a standing-room-only crowd turned out. Suhara Osho began the demonstration with a sharei (ceremonial shooting) followed by a short talk on kyudo. Next, the three of us demonstrated a sequence in which three people take turns shooting at one target. As I waited for our three-person demonstration to begin, I became increasingly anxious. It was very hot, and my hands were sweating. I worried that they would be too wet to grip the bow. I had visions of it slipping from my hands in the middle of the demonstration, embarrassing me in front of family members and friends. However, once we began the demonstration, something happened. As I established my breathing rhythm, a tremendous calm came over me. I felt detached from my concerns and while I did not exactly lose awareness of the audience, for I could still see them and feel their presence, I no longer thought about them. I found myself moving through the steps of the sequence, placing my feet in the proper position without having to think where they should go. While I was not exactly thinking about whether my actions were correct or not, I had the sense that everything was right. I felt that I had abandoned myself to a higher power that was guiding me through the motions. This was the most profound

41

experience that I have had in kyudo. It was the clearest
example of what I understand to be the state of mind one tries
to develop in Zen and the Ways.

There is a saying which emphasizes the role of the proper
state of mind in kyudo. In Japanese it is "Issha Zetsumei." In
my opinion, this saying captures the essential spirit of kyudo.
At Chozen-Ji, this saying is found inscribed over the entrance to
the kyudo dojo, encouraging all to reflect on it every time one
enters to train.

"Issha" translates as one shot, as in the shot of an arrow.
"Zetsumei" translates as "to breathe one's last breath" or, "to
expire." In his book, *Zen Kyudo*, Jackson Morisawa translates
the saying as "One shot (arrow) and expire." The saying
conjures the image of the last act of a dying man; an archer
summarizing his life with one arrow. A more colloquial
translation of the saying, which I have chosen for the title of
this book, is "One arrow, one life."

In discussing Issha Zetsumei, Mr. Morisawa writes, "Each
arrow is final and decisive as each moment is the ultimate."[1]
Time cannot be recaptured. Once a moment is gone, it cannot
be repeated. In Zen, it is recognized that there are no second
chances in life; one strives to pay full attention to each instant,
to every activity no matter how trivial it might seem. One
should throw oneself fully into all activities. Each activity
should be done as if it were one's only activity on Earth. In
kyudo this means to concentrate on every arrow as if it were
the only arrow that the kyudoka will ever shoot.

The state of mind that one endeavors to attain in Zen and
the Zen arts is often referred to as "mushin." It is a compound
word; "mu" means empty, null or void, and "shin" means
heart or mind. It is usually translated as empty mind or no
mind. The closest English concept would probably be uncon-
sciousness, which is not really an accurate translation because
one remains aware of what is happening when one is in
mushin. Suzuki describes mushin as a state in which one is
unconsciously conscious or consciously unconscious.[2] However,

the inseparability of mind and body means that it is misleading to view mushin as a purely mental phenomenon. One cannot reason oneself into mushin; there is no void mind without proper breathing and posture.

A term that is closely related to mushin is samadhi. Originally a Sanskrit word, it refers to a form of intense concentration in which one loses sense of self and other. Actually, mushin and samadhi are probably best thought of as two different aspects of the same phenomenon. There is no mushin without concentration, and intense concentration fosters mushin. Samadhi and mushin are often used more or less interchangeably.

One way to understand mushin is to consider the human stream of consciousness. Most of us have a constant internal dialogue in our minds, perpetuated by a constant chain of associations. This dialogue distracts us from concentrating fully on what we are doing. For example, imagine walking down the street and hearing a noise. Immediately you wonder what the noise is; then you fantasize it is something specific; maybe there was an accident. These thoughts lead to further thoughts, such as thinking about an accident that you saw on the news last night, which leads to thoughts about other news items. Each thought leads to other thoughts; they cloud your awareness of the world. In Zen, such thoughts are referred to as delusions. If you follow them, it is said that you are "attached" to delusions, or that your mind "dwells" on or is "stopped" by them.

In mushin the mind is not distracted by delusive thoughts. Thoughts come and go, but the mind does not dwell on them. The sound of the ambulance is not followed to last night's news. This is the natural state of consciousness and is one of the goals of Zen training. Tanouye Roshi likens mushin to being able to see through one's thoughts as one looks through a propeller. One's experience is pure, unclouded by delusive thought. Consciousness is then free flowing; it moves from object to object, from event to event without being stopped by delusive thoughts. Only then can one treat each moment as the ultimate.

Non-attachment to thoughts and concentration on the moment are amusingly illustrated in the following Zen story about the Zen master, Tanzan, and his disciple, Ekido:

> Tanzan and Ekido were once travelling together down a muddy road. A heavy rain was falling.
> Coming around a bend, they met a lovely girl in a silk kimono and sash, unable to cross the intersection.
> "Come on, girl," said Tanzan at once. Lifting her in his arms, he carried her over the mud.
> Ekido did not speak again until that night when they reached a lodging temple. Then he could no longer restrain himself. "We monks don't go near females," he told Tanzan, "especially not young and lovely ones. It is dangerous. Why did you do that?"
> "I left the girl there," said Tanzan. "Are you still carrying her?"[3]

The idea of concentrating fully on what one is doing is often misunderstood by people without experience in Zen. It does not mean concentrating on one activity to the exclusion of everything else. One does not become so absorbed in what one is doing that one loses awareness of one's surroundings. It is inaccurate to liken samadhi to a person preoccupied with a good book or to a child fixated on the television set. On the contrary, the type of concentration, or samadhi, developed in Zen is such that one has heightened awareness of one's surroundings. There are accounts of monks being able to hear the ashes fall from an incense stick while doing zazen. When one is in the right frame of mind, one's peripheral vision is actually quite large; one has panoramic vision. Tanouye Roshi describes this as seeing 180 degrees. One is acutely aware of one's surroundings but does not dwell on them. In Suzuki's terms, one is consciously unconscious or unconsciously conscious.

Much of our internal dialogue involves thoughts about

ourselves. In mushin one loses this sense of self-awareness and self-reflection. If one is doing something, for example looking at a sunset, one loses the sense that it is "I" who is looking at the sunset just as one loses the internal dialogue telling him how beautiful it is. In mushin, one simply experiences the sunset.

The practice of zazen provides a context which facilitates the student's ability to notice when he is distracted by his internal dialogue. Zazen is usually practiced in a quiet environment in which distracting external stimuli are kept to a minimum. Yet, even without distractions from external sources, the student is easily distracted by the chain of associations going on in his mind. The stillness of the setting makes it easier for him to identify when he becomes attached to delusions. As the student sits, his mind will eventually dwell on extraneous thoughts. At some point, however, he will notice that the thoughts are clouding his perception; they will stand out as unnecessary images on a larger screen of awareness. The recognition that he is dwelling on these thoughts is the cue to adjust his breathing and posture and to focus his attention on counting his breath. Eventually the student can concentrate fully on each breath, allowing him to treat each respiration as an entity in itself. In that way, zazen becomes a vehicle to attain mushin.

The process of kyudo can also be seen as a method to attain mushin through the integration of breathing, posture and concentration. In kyudo, attachment to delusive thoughts is a constant temptation. Any number of delusive thoughts can distract us from full concentration in kyudo. Events or problems in our lives—such as our jobs, financial situations, family lives—can all intrude on concentration. However, the thoughts most difficult to keep from following when one is shooting are those relating to our performance in kyudo itself. Each arrow should be shot without regard to one's past performance or to one's performance in the future, just as Tanzen was able keep from being distracted by the vision of the girl. To do so, one must adjust one's breathing and posture in order to regain one's concentration.

To apply the principle "One arrow, one life" in kyudo is to say that each arrow one shoots and each step in the process of shooting are given unbroken attention. To concentrate on anything else is delusive. While this is easily grasped on an intellectual level, to be able to actually practice it is another matter and takes years of disciplining one's body and mind.

In the practice of kyudo, one shoots countless repetitions of arrows. The same eight steps of shooting are repeated thousands of times. Kyudo is not unique in this degree of repetition. Practitioners of any art or sport must also practice repetitively; expert golf or tennis players also go through thousands of repetitions of their swings. However, in kyudo, one does not make the distinction between practice and "real" performance. The goal is to make every arrow count. That is, every arrow should be shot as if it were the only arrow on Earth; as though one's life were counting on it.

The use of the mato, where a hit or a miss can readily be seen, makes it all the more difficult not to think about one's performance. For example, assume I have done poorly on my last shot. Thoughts of discouragement, embarrassment, or self-reproach might remain with me as I shoot my next arrow. Or, I might be trying to figure out what I did wrong on the previous arrow as I shoot the next. Similarly, let us say that I did well on the previous arrow, a shot that hit the bullseye with a resounding noise for all to hear. Feelings of elation or superiority to the person who shot ahead of me might spring to mind. As I am shooting the next arrow, I might still be thinking about how great I was on the last arrow. Thoughts about future arrows may also come to mind. For example, I might realize that I am holding the bow incorrectly, resolve not to make the same mistake the next time, and start planning the next shot.

In kyudo, a round is usually two arrows, a fact that has definite psychological ramifications. In effect, it makes it harder to maintain mushin. With the second arrow in my right hand as

I shoot the first arrow, the temptation to think about the next shot is greater. Similarly, with the first arrow having hit or missed the target and clearly visible as such, it is all the more difficult not to be thinking about that first shot.

Distractions can arise even in shooting a single arrow. The technical aspects of kyudo are extremely complex; every step is explicitly prescribed—from the position of the arms, to the grip on the bow, to the rhythm of breathing. It is easy to allow one's mind to be stopped by any one aspect of shooting in the middle of a shot. For example, in the process of lifting the bow I might notice that I did not lift it high enough over my head. If my mind continues to dwell on this, if my mind is stopped by this, I will continue to think about that mistake throughout the remainder of the shot.

It is in mushin that one is able to understand the underlying principles of the Universe; that is, ri. The calming of the mind and the freedom from delusive thoughts enables one to experience the world in a different way. This understanding comes as a burst of intuitive insight. In Japanese terms, myo, the wondrous workings of the Universe are revealed. Being in mushin allows the kyudoka to act in accord with the underlying principles of his art.

The understanding that grows out of mushin cannot be seen as limited to cognitive or intellectual understanding. In Zen, any understanding that is not linked to action is considered incomplete. To return to the example of aiming in kyudo that I introduced in the first chapter, mere knowledge or awareness of the precise moment to release the arrow in the cycle of oscillations in aiming is not adequate. One must have that knowledge *and* release the arrow at that same moment. In mushin one acts in the naturally correct way; that is, in accord with the underlying principles. To be able to act in accord with underlying principles, one must lose the sense that one is planning or creating one's actions. Much of the internal dialogue that people have in their minds concerns issues of thinking about and planning what one will do. However, such thoughts are actually delusive. They involve planning for the future and thus keep one from concentrating fully on the present. This can be understood by returning to the example of aiming. If, at the proper moment in the cycle of oscillations, one must say to oneself something like, "I'll shoot it now," it will already be too late in the cycle by the time one releases the arrow. In mushin, one is not attached to thoughts about one's actions. Just as one can watch a sunset without the internal dialogue telling one how beautiful it is, so can one act without the internal dialogue telling one how and when to do it. Then, intuition of the proper time to release the arrow and the release itself coincide.

In *Zen in the Art of Archery*, Herrigel described a state in which:

> Nothing definite is thought, planned, striven for, desired or expected, which aims in no particular direction and yet knows itself capable alike of the possible and impossible . . . this state, which is at bottom purposeless and egoless, was called by the master truly spiritual.[4]

Clearly, Herrigel is referring to the state of mind known as mushin.

In mushin, one unself-consciously acts in accord with the underlying principles of the Universe. Like a third baseman automatically moving his glove to catch a sizzling line drive, there is no interval between thought and action. Suzuki wrote in regards to mushin:

> Psychologically speaking, this state of mind gives itself up unreservedly to an unknown "power" that comes to one from nowhere and yet seems strong enough to possess the whole field of consciousness and make it work for the unknown. He becomes a kind of automaton, so to speak, as far as his consciousness is concerned.[5]

That description could well have been applied to my experience in the demonstration in the Wisconsin State Historical Society Museum.

CHAPTER 4
Koan Zen

If you see a weed, pick it.

Suhara Koun Osho

Students who live at Chozen-Ji are responsible for keeping the buildings and grounds in good order. When I lived there, I was often told that I was passing by areas that needed attention without doing anything about it. On one occasion, Jackson Morisawa noticed three of us relaxing in a yard, oblivious to its state of disarray. He told us, "Suhara Osho says, 'If you see a weed, pick it.' Maybe that's too advanced for you."

The comment was penetrating. In many ways it is a typical Zen statement, simple on the surface but quite deep on another level. On the surface, it underscores the importance of keeping things in order. If something is broken or unsightly, the thing to do is fix it. Thus, we should make our beds, do the dishes, mow our lawns, and paint our houses. To do these things is the naturally correct thing to do. In short, the saying is a good rule to live by.

There is, however, a deeper significance to the comment. In Zen, doing the "right thing" is not in and of itself the ultimate goal. Rather, to do the right things instantly, without any deliberation, is a much higher goal. Simply put, one should not do something merely because one feels that one should do it. That implies conscious deliberation. For example, if I see a weed and I think to myself "There's a weed, I should pick it," the action would be incomplete. The right state of mind would be missing. Even though I might have done the "right thing" it would come from the ego because it involved deliberation. To do it without any conscious deliberation, to do it from mushin, that is point of the saying.

There is a Japanese phrase, "ma o shimeru," which means "to eliminate the space in between." Jackson Morisawa writes about this phrase as follows:

> When the operation of the mind and the body coincide with one point in time and when the space between thought and conduct is eliminated in such a way that they are in perfect unison, we may regard such a moment as the present.[1]

This is the higher level of Suhara Osho's saying, to do the right thing without any space between thought and action.

In Japanese art, the image of the moon reflecting on the water is common. I understand this to symbolize ma o shimeru. Just as the moon instantly hits the water, so should our thoughts and actions be united. The person who lives his life in that fashion is one with his surroundings. He picks the weed as he sees it, without calculation, just as a reflection is made because the light from the moon hits the water. He is the embodiment of the saying. It is an integral part of him, he does not have to give picking weeds any thought; he just does it.

The difference between the two levels of Suhara Osho's comment about picking weeds also applies to the understanding of Zen koans. It will be recalled that a koan is a question posed by a Zen master which is unanswerable by the use of rational logic. This question becomes a focus of concentration for the student. While koans can be approached from an intellectual level, for they do illustrate important concepts in Zen, an intellectual response to the koan is not an acceptable answer. In fact, one of the purposes of using koans as training devices is to break the student's habit of relying on his intellect. Let me give an example.

One of the best known koans in the West is "Joshu's mu." Like many other koans, it originated in an actual dialogue between a Zen master and his disciple. The incident was simple. "A monk once asked Master Joshu, 'Has a dog the Buddha nature or not?' Joshu said, 'Mu.'"[2] The mu of Joshu's answer is the same mu of mushin, meaning null or void. In that sense Joshu seems to give a negative answer to the question.

Kadowaki Kakichi, a Jesuit who became a Zen master after studying with Omori Rotaishi, gives the following explanation of Joshu's mu:

> Buddhism teaches that all beings have the Buddha-nature. But even though doctrinally speaking a dog has the Buddha nature, on the level of common knowledge or practical experience we do not think that this is true. Perhaps the monk thrust this question at Joshu because he was caught in a dilemma between Buddhist doctrine and practical wisdom. Joshu simply answered "Mu!" What does this mean? "Mu" can be translated as "no" or "nothing", but Joshu is not saying that there is no Buddha-nature in a dog. If he were it would be a contradiction of Buddhist teaching, and one of the most eminent masters in Zen history would hardly be denying a fundamental tenet of Buddhism. When he was asked the identical question on another occasion, moreover, the same Joshu answered, "U" [yes]. We can infer, therefore, that this "Mu" transcends both yes and no.[3]

Kadowaki Roshi calls his explanation "armchair theory" as opposed to "living wisdom." He goes on to explain that:

> Mu is to become one with the other and to be concentrated in samadhi so that no matter what you do in daily life, you throw yourself into it body and soul. This is what is meant by understanding mu with the hara and bringing it to life in everyday experience.[4]

Merely talking about the koan is not a true answer to it. An answer to a koan is not an explanation, an answer must be an exemplification. It would be like the difference between explaining the saying "If you see a weed, pick it" and living by it. To demonstrate mu, to be in mushin, that would be a living answer to the Joshu's koan.

Actually, one does not really "give an answer" to a koan; one "becomes the answer." Thus, there is a physical dimension to the answer to a koan. A proper answer must show realization of body and mind; mushin is a state of integration of the physical and the mental. The actual words that one utters when giving an answer to a koan are of secondary importance. One must become the answer in body, mind and action. For this reason, famous answers to koans have been totally nonverbal. For example, when Master Hyakujo wanted to determine which of two students was better suited to become abbot of a monastery, he placed a pitcher on the floor and demanded, "This must not be called a pitcher. What do you call it?" The first monk replied, "It cannot be called a wooden sandal." The second monk kicked the pitcher over and left. The second monk became abbot.[5]

When a Zen student is working on a koan, it becomes the focus of his attention during zazen. In the case of the koan mu, he will repeat "mu" with his breath. If he notices he has lost his concentration, he adjusts his breathing and posture and returns to the koan just as he would if counting his breath. Through this process, an intense samadhi can be built, enabling the student to enter mushin.

Working on a koan is not limited to times when one sits zazen. The same concentration on the koan, the same principles of breathing and posture, should apply in every endeavor. Thus, one strives to maintain mushin in everything that one does. That is why Kadowaki Roshi speaks of bringing mu "into life in everyday experience."

Working on a koan has often been described as a process in which one must transcend a paradox. Many koans manifestly ask the student to give an answer which transcends dualistic thinking. For example, in one koan, a Zen master presents his staff to his disciples and says, "You monks, if you call this a staff, you are committed to the name. If you call this not-a-staff, you negate the fact. Tell me monks, what do you call it?"[6]

In working on a koan, the student must transcend the dualities of thought and non-thought; between purposefulness and purposelessness. The student is asked to give an answer to a seemingly contradictory question. The answer to the koan is mushin; it must come out of mushin. If he is thinking about the answer, he is not in mushin. If he does not think about the koan at all, he is not concentrating on it and then how can he answer it? The way out of this dilemma is to be consciously conscious or unconsciously conscious about the koan. That is, to be in mushin. If the student has in mind the intent to solve the koan, he is engaged in dualistic thinking; he and the koan are separate. However, if he does not have the intent at all of answering the koan, how can he even try? Again, this duality is solved by mushin, a state in which one is intentionally non-intentional or non-intentionally intentional.

Sanzen, the ceremony in which a student presents to his master the answer to his koan, heightens the contradictions involved in working on a koan. At Chozen-Ji, sanzen is held after the evening period of zazen. This sitting is long and the most intense of the day. While sitting, I find it difficult to stop thinking about the fact that I will soon be asked to give my answer to the roshi. Thoughts about the impending meeting intrude. Similarly, it is difficult to not plan my answer in advance. While sitting, I might be mentally rehearsing possible answers. Yet, to be planning an answer in advance is to not be in mushin. In planning an answer, I am already failing to answer the koan.

To give an example of this process, say the student begins the sitting focusing on the koan. In time with his breathing, he thinks "muuuuuuuuuuuu." At some point, thoughts about what to say to the master during sanzen come to mind. If he pursues these thoughts, he is already off track. Without realizing it, he is fantasizing about what to say to the master. Then, suddenly he realizes what he is doing. He has the conscious thought he is not in mushin. This might lead to discouraged thoughts like, "I'll never pass the koan." These thoughts have the potential to generate their own associations, keeping the student further from mushin. Similarly, awareness that he is progressing well on the koan, that he has been in mushin, can also be misleading. Such awareness can generate thoughts like, "Boy, I'm doing really well. I'm really going to show the roshi when I get in the sanzen room." But to have these thoughts, to dwell on the awareness that one is in mushin, is to lose mushin. Only by continually adjusting breathing, posture, and bringing the mind back to the koan can one learn to generate a powerful enough samadhi that one can see through these thoughts.

If, by the end of the sitting, the student has managed to remain in the right frame of mind and body, the process of sanzen presents many hurdles that further test his powers of samadhi to the utmost. At Chozen-Ji, sanzen is announced by the sounding of a bell. The student in charge shouts the command to go and the students jump up and run at full speed out of the meditation hall to form a line behind a bell that is placed on the verandah. The contrast between the silent calm of zazen and the mad dash to the bell can be jarring. To remain in mushin, to retain one's hara during this, is not an easy matter.

When Tanouye Roshi is ready for the first student to come to sanzen, he rings a hand bell. After that, the student strikes the sanzen bell twice with a small wooden mallet. Then he runs at full speed along the verandah until he gets to the room where the roshi is waiting for him.

Ringing the bell twice has the same psychological significance as shooting two arrows in kyudo. Tanouye Roshi says that he can judge the student's frame of mind by the sound he makes when he strikes the sanzen bell. When a student is in the proper frame of mind, the bell gives off a pristine, clear ring. It is common for the student to become attached to the sound he makes with the bell. After a bad hit, thoughts of discouragement or resolution to do better next time might intrude. After a good sounding ring, it is equally easy to become attached to thoughts about that. It takes tremendous concentration to treat each ring as a separate reality.

When the student reaches the sanzen room, he bows, prostrates himself, rises, and enters. Positioning himself before the master, he bows and prostrates himself again. He then tells the master the name of his koan. The master waits for his answer. It is impossible to describe what happens next in a way that does justice to the process. Sanzen is an intense experience that has few parallels. Sitting there, facing his teacher, the student is asked to give a living demonstration of his Zen understanding. Pretense aside, the student must bare his soul. At any time the Master may ring his hand bell, which is the student's signal to bow and leave immediately. Sometimes the student is dismissed before he utters a word. Because of its intensity, sanzen has often been likened to a battle. Zen masters have been known physically to strike their students in sanzen in an attempt to jolt them out of their habitual ways of looking at things.

After the student gives his answer to the koan, several things may happen. The master might ask additional questions that elaborate on the original koan. If the answers are acceptable, he may give a new koan. Or, the master may give the student specific suggestions on how to approach the koan. Or, the student might be summarily dismissed.

The sound of the student being dismissed is the signal to the next student in line to hit the bell and run to the sanzen room. This process is repeated until all the students have gone to sanzen. For the student waiting in line, the length of the wait, and the sight and sound of the other students going to sanzen before him, provide additional stimuli that can lead to distracting thoughts. One must diligently maintain one's breathing, posture, and concentration throughout the wait.

Working on a koan has a dual purpose. First, it is a means to develop and strengthen mushin. The second purpose of koan training is to provide, in sanzen, a formal test of one's progress in Zen. When Zen was at its peak in China and Japan, monasteries were quite large and often had hundreds of monks in training. It was not possible for each of them to have ready access to the Zen master. Sanzen was a way to set aside formally time for the student to meet with a master to have his progress tested and to be guided in his training.

Koans are not limited to questions coming out of the sayings of the old masters. Tanouye Roshi says that any sincere question or problem can become a koan. His students are free to design a koan out of a question from their own life experiences. Physical activities can also be koans. In a story from China, the test of a student's Zen awareness was to ask him to take three steps forward and clear his throat.

Kyudo itself can be viewed as a koan or, perhaps more accurately, as a series of koans where the student is confronted with seemingly paradoxical tasks that can only be resolved by maintaining the right state of mind and body. Consider again the problem of the release of the arrow. It should be a natural, unintentional action. Ideally it occurs when the force of the kyudoka's exhalation expands the chest, pushing the left hand towards the target and pulling the right elbow away from the target. When done correctly, this steadily increasing tension reaches a critical mass which "causes" the string to slip through the kyudoka's gloved fingers, releasing the arrow. The proper release is often likened to snow building up and suddenly slipping off a bamboo leaf.

In kyudo, in contrast to western archery, the string is held deep in the groove formed by the thumb and index finger of the right hand. A leather glove with a reinforced thumb makes this possible. The middle finger rests on the thumb in a position similar to that used when one snaps one's fingers. The index finger rests gently on the middle finger. The string is held in place by both the tension of the middle finger on the thumb and by torque caused by rotating the entire right hand counter-clockwise. The torque helps catch the string in the groove of the glove. At full draw, the force needed to keep the string in the groove is considerable.

Making the release as natural as snow slipping off a leaf is
one of the most difficult challenges of kyudo. It presents the
kyudoka with an apparent paradox between intention and non-
intention, purposefulness and purposelessness. It is possible to
release the arrow by intentionally separating the thumb and
index finger. However, such a purposeful release causes the
string to catch on the glove; this results in a jerky release. If, on
the other hand, the kyudoka consciously tries to keep from
separating his fingers, he runs the risk of not letting go when
the time is right; he will become fatigued and lose his form.
Moreover, he will probably grip the string too tightly, which
will further inhibit the release. If the kyudoka then tries to grip
the string loosely so as better to allow the string to slip through
the groove, he then runs the risk of it slipping out prematurely.

In *Zen and the Art of Archery*, Herrigel discussed, at some
length, the fundamental paradox of the release. After being told
by his teacher that "the shot will go smoothly when it takes the
kyudoka himself by surprise. It must be as if the bowstring
suddenly cut through the thumb that held it," Herrigel wrote
the following:

> If, waiting in vain for the shot, I gave way to the tension
> because it began to be unendurable, then my hands were
> slowly pulled together, and the shot came to nothing. If I
> grimly resisted the tension till I was gasping for breath, I
> could only do so by calling on the arm and shoulder
> muscles for aid. I then stood there immobilized—like a
> statue.[7]

Mushin, not technique, solves the paradox of the release.
Mushin allows one to transcend technique and intuit the
naturally correct way of letting the string release itself from the
hand. In this way, the release is neither purposeful nor
purposeless. This can only be accomplished by maintaining
mushin; there must be a union of breathing, posture, and
concentration at full draw.

At kai, there are two major lines of force in the body.

A vertical line is formed by the downward pressure of the breath and the raising of the spine. Simultaneously, a horizontal line of force is formed by the expansion of the chest and the outward pressure of the legs. As he holds the arrow at kai, the kyudoka concentrates on adjusting his breathing and posture so the vertical and horizontal lines of force meet at right angles. At that point we say that one is in the center of the "perfect cross." The process of concentrating on establishing the cross is referred to as the "inner aim" of kyudo; the kyudoka seeks to create his spiritual center by reaching the center of the perfect cross. According to Jackson Morisawa, when the center of the perfect cross is reached, "one becomes one with the bow, the arrow, and the target (Universe)."[8] Mushin will prevail. The koan of the release will be solved and myo, the wondrous workings of the Universe, will be revealed as the kyudoka permits the string to slip from his glove like snow sliding off a bamboo leaf.

At Chozen-Ji, students of kyudo are given formal koans to present to Tanouye Roshi during sanzen. However, on a deeper level, the student comes to see his formal koan and his kyudo as being one and the same. Working on a koan during zazen and working towards a natural release in kyudo are methods of training that complement each other. Both are ways of developing and sustaining mushin. Through zazen, because one is relatively still, one can deepen one's samadhi powers. Kyudo offers a systematized method of training to maintain that samadhi while engaged in activity.

Early in my training, Tanouye Roshi explained that as I improved in kyudo my zazen (and progress on my koan) would improve. Conversely, as my zazen improved, so would my kyudo. I see my kyudo and my koan as being separate, but interlocked, parts of the same whole. But having Zen understanding only when sitting cross-legged or when shooting an arrow is not adequate. To have the same understanding when one is engaged in everyday activities is what is really important, for all activities are part of that same whole. Thus, picking a weed as naturally as snow falls off a bamboo leaf is an expression of the Zen awareness. Seeing a weed and being able simply to pick it without "any space in between" is in itself a koan of profound significance.

CHAPTER 5

The Naturally Correct Way

You have to learn how to push the rock where it wants to go.

Tanouye Tenshin Roshi

When I arrived at Chozen-Ji, the temple was in the midst of a major construction project. In the middle of the two and one half acre grounds is a hill where one day will be the main meditation hall. When I first arrived, the only things on the hill were eucalyptus trees and rocks. The next day we began to clear the hill for construction.

Physical labor has always played an important role in traditional Zen training. In fact, the first rule of monastery life is "A day of no work is a day of no eating."[1] Labor is necessary to support the monasteries, but becomes a form of moving zazen when the student refines his breathing, posture and concentration while doing vigorous labor. In that way he learns to maintain mushin in all circumstances.

At Chozen-Ji, zazen, martial arts practice, and physical labor are complementary components of training. During my first stay at Chozen-Ji we arose at 4.30 a.m. and worked from approximately 7.00 a.m. until 4.00 p.m. with time out for lunch. I would practice kyudo after evening zazen. Tanouye Roshi worked along side during the day and often instructed in Zen as we worked. One of my first lessons occurred on my first full day at Chozen-Ji.

Four of us were clearing rocks off the hill to make a path. Some of these rocks were large and difficult to move. My approach to the work was simple and direct. I decided where I wanted to move a rock, then pushed it in that direction. Unfortunately, I made very little headway and quickly exhausted myself.

Tanouye Roshi watched me with considerable amusement. Finally he interceded. He explained I was trying to impose my will on the rocks; I was trying to make them go where I wanted them to go. "You have to learn how to push the rock where it wants to go," he told me. He explained further that, if I could do that, I could coax the rocks to where I wanted them to go. He then showed me that, because rocks are unevenly shaped, there is usually one direction in which, if pushed, the rock is easier to unbalance and flip over. He told me that I must learn how to utilize the direction in which the rock "wanted" to go in order to move it where I wanted it to go. This would result in considerably less expenditure of effort on my part, he assured me.

Tanouye Roshi explained further that this principle is central to the martial arts. In judo, for example, one does not push or pull an opponent in a direction against which he is well braced for an attack. Rather, one looks for an imbalance, a direction to push or pull in which the opponent will easily be knocked off balance. Many times this state of being off balance is caused by the opponent's own momentum, and the technique of pushing or pulling the opponent in the direction he is already moving (wants to go) is the easiest way to unbalance him.

Actually I was already familiar with this principle from my previous martial arts experiences. But I never thought these principles could be applied to an activity such as moving rocks. At that time I still viewed martial arts as ways to develop technical proficiency in specific activities. I did not see them as Ways—true Zen arts. To study a Way, one must approach it as a road to spiritual awakening. In the process one must understand that the principles learned in the art are applicable to everyday life.

At the end of his talk, Tanouye Roshi demonstrated a way to find out where a rock "wanted" to go. He put his hand on one edge of the rock and tipped it slowly. He then put his hand on another part and repeated this process. This continued until he had pushed the rock at several points around its circumference. Next he showed me the point at which it was easiest to push the rock. By pushing that point, he effortlessly moved the rock in the direction it "wanted" to go. He continued to demonstrate how, by repeating the process of pushing the rock in its favored direction and occasionally spinning the rock so as to reorient the direction it "wanted" to go, it was quite easy to move it where I wanted it to go.

I went back to my work of moving rocks. I carefully studied each rock, pushed it in numerous places and tried to find the way the rock "wanted" to move. Sometimes I was successful and the rock moved quite easily. At other times, I was unable to find the favored direction of the stone. Sometimes this was because the rock was too heavy for me to try tipping it. At such times, I tried to reason which was the best direction in which to push it. Typically, however, I failed.

When I later discussed these difficulties with Tanouye Roshi, he explained that my approach to the task was too intellectual; that I was relying too much on my ego—that is, my conscious mind—to figure out which way the stone "wanted" to move. While tipping the rock was often helpful, it is only a technique and therefore not applicable to all situations. To understand how to move a rock, I had to "throw away" my ego and "become one" with the rock. The proper direction would then be readily apparent, as a burst of intuition. To experience this, I had to be in the right frame of mind.

I later realized that Tanouye Roshi was explaining the differences between ri and ji in moving rocks. It will be recalled from Chapter 1 that ri refers to underlying principles and ji to specific manifestations of those principles or techniques. Ri is formless and unchanging. Ji will vary from situation to situation. The Roshi was telling me that the underlying principle was to find the way the rock naturally "wanted" to move. The specific manifestations of the principle will vary from rock to rock, from terrain to terrain. So, too, will the specific techniques for determining the proper direction vary from situation to situation. I had learned one technique, tipping the rock at various points. In some instances it was successful and led to more efficient action. I also realized that Tanouye Roshi was explaining to me that the way to grasp the underlying principle is to be in mushin; then realization of the proper way to move the rock would come as a burst of intuition.

In Japanese, when an action is considered to not be in accord with ri—the underlying principles—it is referred to as "muri". Pushing a rock in a direction it did not "want" to go would be muri. Doing something in accord with ri is the naturally correct way of doing it. It leads to more efficient, more powerful, and more aesthetically pleasing results. For any activity, there are ways to do it that are naturally correct and ways to do it that are muri. It is as if there are invisible creases in the Universe. These creases correspond to ri, principles. To do something that is in accordance with principles is to fold neatly along those creases. To do something that is muri is to force a fold against the lines of those natural creases.

In discussing these terms, Leggett wrote:

> To do something "muri" or without ri is to force a result, using unnatural and therefore ultimately wasteful and tiring means. To shout someone down in an argument, to use advantages of wealth, prestige or physical strength to override the legitimate interests of others, to chop wood against the grain, to bang the keys of a typewriter—all of these are examples of muri. It has been said that doing things muri is doing things without love for the material at hand. To do things in conformity with ri is to feel oneness of self with them.[2]

The first time that I heard Tanouye Roshi use the term muri we were clearing timber. In order to load logs on the truck, we had to cut them into more manageable pieces. We used four chainsaws to do this. Workers without the saws hauled the wood to the truck. While some of us were cutting, the others were hauling; Tanouye Roshi sharpened saw blades as they became dull.

I was one of the sawyers. As I worked, I noticed that it was taking me much longer to cut through a trunk than other people. I checked the saw blade and found it dull. I took the saw to Tanouye Roshi; he sharpened it. I returned to my sawing. I again noticed it took me longer to cut than the others. I thought that I was not applying enough downward pressure on the saw, and bore down harder on the blade. It cut no quicker. I checked the blade again. It was dull. I took it back to Tanouye Roshi; he sharpened it again. This entire process was repeated several times.

After sharpening my blade three or four times, compared with only once for the other students, Tanouye Roshi took me aside. Sitting me down on a large rock and shaking his head from side to side with a mixture of sympathy and disbelief he said, "Ken, in Japanese there is a very important word: muri. Have you ever heard of it?"

I had heard of it but, out of embarrassment, I remained silent. He went on to tell me my use of the chainsaw was muri. He pointed out that I was not keeping the saw perpendicular to the wood. As a result, the blade was not approaching the wood at the proper angle, and was therefore cutting inefficiently. My heavy touch, combined with the wrong angle of attack, accelerated the wear on the saw blade. Tanouye Roshi then showed me the proper way to use the saw. He stressed the importance of keeping the blade perpendicular to the wood. If the angle was correct and the blade was sharp, the weight of the saw would provide sufficient pressure to cut the wood in accord with the way the saw was meant to cut. Demonstrating, he held the saw in one hand without bearing down on the blade. The saw cut cleanly with little effort. He then showed me how to hold the saw to keep the blade perpendicular to the wood. He suggested holding it as if it were a sword in kendo.

Demonstrating, he held the sword in front of him and told me that it was important to keep my feet spread, my head and back straight. He told me to breath from my hara and to let the force of my breath press on the saw. "Concentrate," he said. "Become one with the saw." I tried the posture and found that it worked. As a result, I was able to cut more efficiently without dulling the blade.

When Tanouye Roshi first explained the principle behind moving rocks, I assumed he was only giving me advice on how to make that particular labor easier. One day, four of us were faced with the task of moving a very large stone, a boulder so large that it took all of us to move it. We took turns deciding which way it should be moved. Three of us were college-educated professionals: a psychologist, a social worker and a kinesiologist. Each tried and failed. Then, the fourth student, a high-school dropout with emotional problems easily directed us on the proper way to move the rock. Tanouye Roshi, observing this, laughed. He said that we professionals were thinking too much; our egos were keeping us from "becoming one with" the rock. The high-school boy succeeded because he was not using his ego as much as we were. The Roshi chided further: if we had truly understood the basic principles of our professions, we would have known how to move the rock with the least effort. "Ken," he said, "approach the rock as if you're doing psychotherapy with it."

Later I talked with Tanouye Roshi about his last comments. He said there should be no difference between moving rocks and my field, psychotherapy. Both involve movement, the facilitation of change. One does not want to push directly against resistance. Rather, one tries to push in the direction of least resistance. Trying to force change on a patient is like pushing a rock where it does not "want" to go; both are muri, and therefore inefficient. To do so in psychotherapy can easily raise the patient's resistance. Instead, one must look for the direction of least resistance. This can be the direction in which a person is most ready to change or, at the least, a direction against which they are not strongly defending. The process should begin at that point. Psychotherapy and moving rocks share an underlying principle. By learning how to move rocks and by learning how to unbalance a person physically I would improve my skills as a psychotherapist.

Tanouye Roshi's comments about psychotherapy surprised me in a way that his connections between judo and moving rocks did not. Moving rocks and judo both involve, at least superficially, physical movement. Further, I knew that he had considerable experience doing manual labor like this and it stood to reason that one would pick up the techniques of moving rocks with experience. But the philosophical connection between moving rocks and psychotherapy was not at all obvious to me.

Tanouye Roshi's comments about psychotherapy were surprisingly accurate. There is a school of psychotherapy, usually referred to the school of "strategic therapy," whose adherents avoid directly confronting a patient's resistance. At times the therapist will even avoid talking directly about a patient's symptoms. Instead, they rely on strategies that push the patient along the path of least resistance.

The originator of the strategic school was a psychiatrist, Milton Erickson. A good example of this approach is found in the following account:

> When Erickson was on the staff of Worcester State Hospital, there was a young patient who called himself Jesus. He paraded about as the Messiah, wore a sheet draped around him, and attempted to impose Christianity on people. Erickson approached him on the hospital grounds and said, "I understand you've had experience as a carpenter?" The patient could only reply that he had. Erickson involved the young man in a special project and shifted him to productive labor.[3]

Apparently, the patient was so well prepared to resist doctors who tried to convince him that he was not the messiah that it was easy to unbalance him by accepting his position. Erickson was able to engage him in productive work by pushing him in a direction against which he was not prepared to resist.

Tanouye Roshi has no formal training in psychotherapy and, to my knowledge, had read little on the subject. Because of his training, he could see the underlying principles shared by judo, moving rocks and psychotherapy. There are many Zen stories in which a master is able to promote profound psychological change in people by making seemingly simple comments or actions. These comments, or actions, have such profound impact because they are aimed precisely at the person's most receptive areas for change. They unbalance the person because they push him in ways against which there is minimal resistance; they fold neatly along the invisible creases. Profound changes can thus be promoted with minimal effort on the teacher's part. The following story is but one example from Zen literature of a master effortlessly producing psychological change by applying pressure in the right direction:

A teacher was having a meal with two pupils of some years' standing, a man and woman. The man knew that the woman, who had a witty tongue, occasionally used to make amusing but biting comments at the expense of others, and he suspected that she was not above inventing some details to give an extra edge to the little aggressions. Though generally likable and kind-hearted, she could not resist taking an occasional opening which presented itself.

During the meal, the teacher suddenly launched into a stream of vicious criticisms of someone well-known to all of them, producing wild slanders and accusations which they knew to be untrue. After a little, the two pupils cried out in protest, "Oh teacher, you *can't* say that." The teacher's flow stopped as if a tap had been turned off; after a little silence he began calmly to speak of something else.

The two went home thoughtfully. After some weeks, the

man noticed that the woman was very careful about her comments in regard to other people; in particular, she never gave rein to her talent for impromptu sarcasms. He realized that she had seen herself in what the teacher had done; he had held up a mirror before her, and because she had done some training, she had been able to realize that it was a reflected image, and not a characteristic of the mirror itself. He thought how privileged he had been to be a witness of this spiritually inspired instruction.

A fault, he pondered, of which she had been entirely unconscious, had been brought to light without direct criticism, which might have made her defensive. But how extraordinary that she could have been so completely unaware of it before. Then he thought, I should not take this as applying to her alone; I should reflect whether I myself have ever at all offended in the same respect. Hardly—I make jokes, of course, but no one could resent . . . well, perhaps once. No—twice . . . No, more than that . . . oh dear, dear dear. And now he thought that perhaps it had been she who had been privileged to be witness of spiritually inspired instruction.[4]

To put this discussion of the "naturally correct way" in the context of the kyudo, I will return once again to the release. Earlier, I explained that the proper release is a manifestation of mushin and thus neither intentional nor non-intentional; it should be like snow slipping off a bamboo leaf. There is another saying that captures the feeling of the proper release: "Like a heavy drop of water that decides to be free, the arrow liberates itself."[5] The correct release of the string from the glove allows the arrow to be liberated naturally from the string, without interference on the part of the kyudoka.

The drawing of the bow takes starts at the end of the stage called uchiokoshi (lifting the bow). At that point, the kyudoka's arms are almost fully extended away from his body. The bow is held over the head so that his arms and body form a 45-degree angle (see illustration, p. 22). In the first part of the stage called hikiwaki (drawing the bow), the kyudoka draws the bow one-third by pushing his left hand towards the target. This motion pulls the right hand towards the target, forcing the elbow to bend at a right angle. This position is known as daisan (the great third). The grip on the bow is firmly established at daisan. After a slight pause, the bow is drawn fully by the thrust of the left hand towards the target and the pull of the right elbow in the opposite direction. In the process, the bow is lowered and brought towards the kyudoka's body until the arrow is touching his cheek, even with his mouth. This begins the stage of kai, in which the drawing tension is steadily increased as the kyudoka seeks to establish the perfect cross.

Because the kyudoka does not let the bow grip slip in his hands as the bow is brought from a position in which it is extended from the body (daisan) to one in which it is held close to his body (kai), torque on the grip is created. The bow strains, like a coiled string, to rotate counter-clockwise. This torque creates an additional source of power: when the arrow is released, the bow naturally spins counter-clockwise in the kyudoka's hand, adding additional thrust.

Throughout kai, the kyudoka's gloved right hand must restrain an increasing amount of potential energy as the expansion of his chest increases both the drawing pressure on the bow and the torque on the grip. At some point, the critical mass of tension is reached which should allow the string to slip naturally out of the kyudoka's gloved hand. If the arrow is allowed to slip from the glove at the proper moment, it will release, without impediment, the potential energy contained within the drawn bow. This will result in a true flight of the arrow. However, if the kyudoka consciously tries to effect the release, his timing will be off and the string will not slip naturally from his glove. This will inhibit the release of energy, which will be reflected in the flight of the arrow. To be able to intuit the proper instant, one must be in proper balance of body and mind; that is, in mushin. When the perfect cross is reached, the kyudoka functions as a conduit for the natural liberation of the arrow; the kyudoka, the bow and the arrow will be one.

In Zen, students strive to accord with ri in everything that they do. This is true whether they are moving rocks, preparing dinner, picking weeds, hauling garbage to the dump or washing dishes. In every activity, one tries to find the invisible creases. At Chozen-Ji, the Zen art or arts that one studies can be seen as areas of specialization. They provide structured, proven ways of learning how to find the underlying principles in circumscribed activities. However, the real challenge is to apply the principles of the Zen arts in activities outside of the dojo and to find the naturally correct ways of doing things in everyday life.

CHAPTER 6
Zanshin

The string has a life of its own.

Tanouye Tenshin Roshi

Towards the end of my first stay at Chozen-Ji, I spent an afternoon working with Tanouye Roshi on a drainage ditch alongside a road at the back of the temple. As he dug the ditch with a backhoe, I followed with a shovel, removing loose dirt and measuring the depth of the ditch to ensure that it ran on a slight downhill grade. The measurements were made with a piece of string given to me by the Roshi. After making the first measurement, I crumpled up the string and put it in my pocket. When the time came for the next measurement, I pulled the wadded string out of my pocket, untangled it, and made the measurement. Afterward, without thinking, I returned the string to my pocket and resumed shoveling. When time came to make the next measurement, I had to untangle the string again. After several measurements, I stopped putting the string in my pocket and put it on the ground. Then I had trouble finding it in the tall grass; and when I found it, it was still tangled. On a few occasions I lost it altogether and had to find more string.

My disorganization was slowing down the progress of our work. After a while this became critical because a storm started to move into the valley. If we did not finish the ditch before the rain, the area, especially the kyudo dojo, would flood. When Tanouye Roshi saw me start untangling the string one more time, he got off the tractor, picked up a small bamboo stick lying on the ground, took the string from me, wrapped it around the stick, and handed the assembly to me. The device kept the string from tangling and was easier to keep track of. He then turned to me and said, "What's the matter with you? Don't you see that the string has a life of its own? You're killing it! Would you treat a bowstring that way?" We resumed our work and barely finished the ditch on time. I never lost or tangled the string again.

I have thought a lot about this incident over the years. It illustrates one of the most important principles as well as one of the most important problems in the study of the Ways. We study the Zen arts to learn their principles and how to apply them to all spheres of life. There is, however, a certain seductiveness to the arts; it is easy to lose the larger perspective and treat the arts as ends in themselves. We call this attachment to the form of the art. Tanouye Roshi's comment had such impact on me because it pointed out how overly attached I had become to the form of kyudo. He was right, I would not have treated a bowstring that way.

The eighth stage in hassetsu, the shooting sequence, is called zanshin. Zanshin is an important term in the Ways. Zan can be translated as remaining, or lingering. Shin translates as either heart or mind. Zanshin is often referred to as "follow-through," but this is something of a trivialization. On a deeper level, zanshin means that the state of mind and body used in executing an action is not dissipated by it, but is carried over into the next activity. On a physical level, breathing and posture remain correct; the body remains in balance and ready to move again. On a mental level, one's awareness and concentration remain. Anyone who has seen a samurai movie will recognize the portrayal of zanshin as the composed, balanced, and alert attitude that a warrior maintains when, immediately after striking down one assailant with his sword, he is poised to strike the next one. Zanshin is not limited to the martial arts. In calligraphy, for example, the energy of one character does not stop at the end of the stroke, but rather continues into the next.

This stage, zanshin, is illustrated in the last of the drawings of hassetsu in Chapter 1 (p. 27). From the standpoint of posture, zanshin is the position the body naturally assumes after the correct release. The force of the release thrusts the kyudoka's right hand backwards in a straight line, pivoting at the elbow. As the chest reaches maximal expansion, the left arm is thrust forward and to the left. If the kyudoka does not interfere with the natural motions generated by the release, at zanshin the arms will be extended to the sides, creating the form of a cross with the body. The head remains turned toward the target and the shoulders are relaxed. The stance remains unchanged: feet spread wide, pelvis thrust forward, back and neck in their natural positions. The position is held for the duration of an unhurried inhalation, then the hands are brought back to the hips. While it is relatively easy to mimic zanshin by intentionally moving the arms to the appropriate position, proper zanshin is an unintentional, natural action.

On a mental level, the kyudoka must, at the stage of zanshin, come to terms with the quality of the shot. One sees clearly whether or not the arrow hit the target. However, one should not dwell on the completed shot. If he does, his concentration will lapse. Zanshin, then, is the pivotal phase during which it is determined whether the shot just completed will haunt the kyudoka like the memory of the young girl being carried over the mud or whether he will be able to maintain void mind.

The quality of one's breath is critical in determining whether one can maintain correct posture and concentration. As I have already explained, the release of the arrow is powered by the breath. At the stage of kai, the kyudoka bears down on his hara with his breath. Simultaneously, he lifts the nape of his neck as he seeks to align all the elements necessary to create the perfect cross. The downward pressure of the breath and the extension of the spine cause his chest to expand. This, in turn, pushes the left hand towards the target and pulls the right elbow backward. In the process, the tension of the draw is increased steadily throughout kai. Finally, a critical mass of tension is achieved and the string naturally, and unintentionally, slips through the fingers of the glove.

The arrow's release sends a tremendous burst of energy through the body. If the kyudoka's breathing is incorrect, both the body and mind are jolted. When this happens, chances are that the kyudoka has either held his breath or has expelled it during the release, but in such a way that dissipates the energy in the hara. In either case, he must gasp for breath after the release of the arrow. Such improper breathing is accompanied by a break in concentration as, for an instant, the kyudoka loses awareness of the release.

If one's breathing and posture are correct, the energy generated by the release is dispersed throughout the body, as the kyudoka inhales without interruption of the rhythm of his breathing. One maintains awareness throughout; there is no lapse in concentration. In *Zen in the Art of Archery*, Herrigel describes the difference between right and wrong shots as follows:

> After wrong shots the pent-up breath is expelled explosively, and the next breath cannot be drawn quickly enough. After the right shots the breath glides effortlessly to its end, whereupon air is unhurriedly breathed in again. The heart continues to beat evenly and quietly, and with concentration undisturbed you can go straight to the next shot.[1]

Ideally, zanshin refers to continuity of mushin after the release of the arrow. However, zanshin can also refer to a recovery from a poorly executed shot, one in which mushin was lost. If the kyudoka is able to restore proper breathing, posture, and concentration after a poor shot, one would also call this good zanshin. Everybody will have bad shots; everyone will lose the proper balance of body and mind; the important thing is to recover as quickly as possible. In this sense, zanshin refers to the restoration of mushin after losing it.

Just as it is possible to have good zanshin after a bad shot, it is possible to have bad zanshin after a good shot. Losing one's breath after an otherwise good shot or becoming attached to having shot well, are examples of losing zanshin.

Perhaps the greatest test of zanshin is when the string, or the bow itself, breaks in the middle of a shot. During full draw, it is a startling experience. Until that happened to me, I did not realize the force that a bow generates. The first time I had a string break, I instinctively jumped back and threw my bow to the ground with a crash. When the string breaks on a master kyudoka, he does not flinch at all. He remains composed, keeping his arms extended as if the arrow had been shot. Afterward, he gracefully brings his arms to his hips and bows as he normally would. His breathing, posture and concentration are uninterrupted; composure is never lost.

Thus, in kyudo, zanshin is the continuity of spirit at the end of a shot. It enables the kyudoka to maintain the proper state of mind and body from shot to shot. There is another, more profound, level to zanshin: continuity of spirit outside the kyudo dojo. In this regard, Jackson Morisawa writes: "The remaining heart also means that one must carry over the kyudo principles into one's daily life."[2]

In Zen we say that there is no inside and there is no outside. Thus, there should be no distinction between inside the Dojo and outside the Dojo. Issha Zetsumei applies equally beyond the physical confines of the training hall. One should approach all activities and situations with the same sincerity, the same intensity, and the same awareness that one has with bow and arrow in hand. One learns how to attain mushin while shooting arrows in order to maintain it in one's everyday life.

Understanding that there should be no distinction between the inside and the outside of the dojo is one thing; living that way is another. The dojo is a controlled environment, designed to foster mushin. For that reason it is removed from the commotion of daily life. Dojo protocol restricts unnecessary talk and movement in order to keep the students from being distracted. Students are expected to maintain proper posture while in the dojo and those who slouch are likely to be reprimanded. Beginning students have teachers and advanced students as role models; they set the standards of behavior. In the dojo, the student has bow and arrow in hand; these are the ultimate tools with which he forges mushin. When the student leaves the dojo, he leaves behind those aspects of the dojo which help him attain and maintain mushin. He alone is responsible for maintaining correct breathing, posture, and concentration. He must carry the spirit of the dojo with him. This is a heavy load to bear in the "real world." Eventually mushin will dissipate. He will become immersed in the activities and problems of daily life and will forget to monitor his breathing, posture and concentration. Further, if he notices he has lapsed, he might feel too discouraged to try to correct himself; he knows that he has picked up the burden of the dojo many times in the past, only to drop it again. However, if he keeps on trying, his stamina will increase. He will increase the distance he can carry the load and the load will become easier to lift. Increasingly, he should be able to maintain mushin in his daily life. Seen thus, zanshin is both carrying the spirit of the dojo into the real world and the willingness to pick it up again after dropping it.

The student of the Way has unlimited opportunity to re-establish right breathing, posture, and concentration in his daily activities. For example, as a psychotherapist, I conduct as many as eight therapy sessions per day. It is my responsibility to pay full attention to whomever I am seeing at the time. Yet extraneous thoughts can intrude. Thoughts about past or future appointments come to mind. Distractions can also involve my home life, my financial situation, world events, and what I want to eat for lunch. To pursue these thoughts, to let my mind "stop" on them only interferes with my ability to help the person before me. To live the principle "one arrow, one life" would be to free myself from such distractions. In order to work towards that goal, I am becoming increasingly aware of my breathing and posture while I am working. As in kyudo and in zazen, I try to adjust my breathing and posture to bring myself back to the present moment when I notice that I am distracted.

There are many variations of this same theme in everyday life. How many times do you forget what you are doing in the middle of an activity because you are thinking about something else? How many times are you half listening to someone while you are actually thinking about something else? How often are you distracted as you talk to someone at a party because you are trying to figure out how to meet a more interesting or more attractive person? How many times do you sit down to eat a meal and start thinking about the next one? Most people will probably think this is just human nature and cannot be overcome. However, the underlying premise of Zen and the Ways is that it is possible to overcome such attachments. In studying kyudo we strive to treat every event as an entity in itself, without distraction. By learning how to regulate breathing and posture, one tries to learn to see through such delusive thoughts in order to be fully present moment by moment.

When the student is able to sustain mushin in daily life, he is able to see the ri, the underlying principles, of everyday life. He is able to see the invisible folds of the Universe and do daily activities the "naturally correct way." This enables him to become aware of the life in all things. Most of us go through life oblivious to the folds of the universe; we habitually trample out the life of things around us, just as I murdered the string. Ultimately, one studies a Way to learn to see the natural order—the life—in everyday things. The activity of a Way is a microcosm, a controlled environment, in which one is able to refine one's "psycho-physical apparatus" so one can see the naturally correct way of performing a specific activity. In kyudo, we learn the naturally correct way of shooting an arrow; in tea ceremony, one learns the naturally correct way of serving tea; in flower arrangement, one learns the naturally correct way of arranging flowers. In so doing, one learns to see the life of the bow and arrow, the tea kettle and cup, and the flowers and vase. These activities become elevated to Ways when the student strives to extend mushin outside the dojo so that one can see the naturally correct way of leading one's life. As the student's zanshin increases, as he is better able to maintain mushin outside the dojo, he will increasingly go through life killing less of the life around him.

The concept of zanshin separates the Ways from the artistic and athletic traditions in the West. Mastery of the underlying principles of an art is not unique to the Zen arts and is found in Western arts as well. So, too, is mushin found in the Western cultural traditions. I have found that Western musicians and dancers to whom I have explained the concept of ri, ji, and mushin readily understand them and describe experiences in which the art "took over" and they performed without self-awareness. Suzuki discusses the experience of a master bullfighter as an example of mushin.[3] In the West, however, inspiration in the performance of an art is seen as the end point. The concept of treating the art as a microcosm of life is unique to the Ways.

CHAPTER 7

Pain

The pain isn't getting worse, your tolerance for it is getting less.

Tanouye Tenshin Roshi

One of the high points in every student's Zen training is an event called sesshin. "Sesshin" literally means "collecting of the spirit" and is a marathon training retreat. For a period lasting from two days to a week, students get together for intensive training. They participate in zazen for much of the day and night with very little sleep. Because of its intensity, one sesshin is equivalent to a much longer period of regular training.

Tanouye Roshi used to come to Chicago once or twice a year to conduct sesshin for his students on the mainland. It was at one of these sesshin that I first met him. I had gone there with trepidation. I had little confidence in my ability to sustain zazen for long periods of time, and knew this would cause problems. At sesshin students are required to participate in all of the zazen periods; one cannot decline to participate when things get difficult. Further, leaving in the middle of the sesshin is very bad form.

From the beginning, I found zazen an extremely painful process. For as long as I could remember, I avoided sitting cross-legged on the floor because I found it too uncomfortable. My hip and leg muscles were tight; I could only assume an awkward version of the tailor's position, with my legs remaining high off the ground. It was very uncomfortable for more than a brief period of time.

I first attempted zazen in Mike Sayama's apartment. I had

never been interested in zazen before, but Mike had made it a required part of training. He showed me the basics of zazen and I tried to get into a half-lotus position. My body was so stiff that I could not even come close. Instead, I got into my version of the tailor's position and sat that way for half an hour. It seemed like forever. My knees did not rest on the ground, so they cramped after a short period. In addition, because the position was so unstable, I had to use a fair amount of effort to keep from toppling over.

About six months later I went to my first sesshin with Tanouye Roshi. Over that time my body had hardly loosened up at all. My knees were still off the ground, and it was still uncomfortable sitting. We had done some "mini-sesshin" in Michigan and I had considerable difficulty sitting through them. I knew that the Chicago sesshin would be a test of my determination to study Zen.

After the first few sittings, the pain grew progressively worse. By the second day I felt intense pain within a few minutes of taking my position. Since movement is not permitted during zazen, I was unable to shift position to ease the pain. Instead of concentrating on breathing, posture and counting my breaths, my attention went into restraining myself from crying out or moving around. Sometimes I tried to distract myself by thinking about things other than the pain. Other times I tried to fall asleep to escape the pain. But the pain made escape seem impossible.

During the breaks in zazen, I talked to Tanouye Roshi about my difficulties. While he made it clear that most people find zazen difficult, at least in the beginning, he assured me that there was nothing to worry about; I could not injure myself doing zazen. He encouraged me to keep at it and not give up. "Take your pain up by your hara," he would tell me. I would smile politely, not yet believing there was such a thing as a hara.

By the third and last day of the sesshin, I was desperate. The pain continued to grow. Each time I took my place for zazen I was convinced that I would not be able to get up again. I had visions of walking around as a cripple. I became intensely jealous of those people more flexible than I who appeared to have no difficulties sitting. I knew that what I was doing was not really zazen, for in zazen you are supposed to feel calm and be free of thoughts. All I was doing was trying to think of thoughts to distract me from the pain. Finally, during one of the last breaks, hoping for some secret to make the pain go away, I again expressed my concern and frustration to Tanouye Roshi. I explained that whatever I did, the pain continue to worsen. Instead of giving me a way to reduce the pain he said, "The pain isn't getting worse, your tolerance of it is getting less."

I felt disappointed. Hoping that he would tell me some trick to ease the pain or at least reassure me that the pain would go away, Tanouye Roshi was telling me to learn to live with it. Anyway, I did not really believe him. I was convinced that the pain was, in fact, getting worse. Stifling the urge to leave the sesshin and quit Zen training, I forced myself to continue.

Then, during one of the last rounds of zazen, something happened. By then the pain was so great that I was leaning backwards in order to take some of the weight off my legs. Tanouye Roshi walked around the hall as we sat in order to inspect our postures. As he came near me, I resolved to sit properly, without slouching, regardless of the pain. Just when he came in front of me, I suddenly felt detached from the pain. I cannot say that I did not feel the pain any less, but it did not bother me as much. It was as though I had accepted the pain and was able to tolerate it. That tolerance lasted through the end of sesshin. Afterwards I realized that Tanouye Roshi was right: my tolerance of the pain was the problem, not the pain itself.

In spite of having left the Chicago sesshin encouraged to continue practicing zazen, my difficulties with it were only beginning. While I was able to assume a rough variation of a half-lotus, it was as painful as my earlier posture. Then, about a year later, I injured my knee which made sitting cross-legged even more difficult. Because of that, I did zazen in the seiza position (sitting on the knees with feet tucked under the buttocks) for about a year after that. The posture was less painful for short periods of time. However, because everyone else was sitting in the half-lotus and lotus positions, I continued to see that as my goal.

When I went to Chozen-ji the first time, I felt that I was at a choice point. My knee had healed to the point where I thought it was safe to sit cross-legged. I felt that if I did not begin sitting cross-legged soon, it would become more difficult to do as I got older. So I began sitting in my version of the half-lotus.

Zazen at Chozen-Ji brought unexpected difficulties. The evening sitting is comprised of two forty-five-minute periods. I had not sat cross-legged for over year, and I was quite stiff. After the first few nights, I had something happen to me that I had never experienced before. About halfway into the second sitting, my body tensed up and began to shake uncontrollably. Nothing I did could control the shaking for more than a few minutes. This was highly irregular behavior in a Zen temple, where no gross movements are permitting during zazen.

In Zen temples, the person who is in charge of the sitting is called the jikijitsu. During the sittings he walks around carrying a light wooden stick, called a keisaku, which he uses to rap students on their backs. The blow relieves cramping and focuses the student's attention. The student may request a hit by pressing his palms together when the jikijitsu walks in front of him. In the Rinzai tradition, the jikijitsu has the option of striking the student without being asked to do so if he feels that it will help the student keep still or concentrate better. On seeing me shake, the jikijitsu came and rapped me with the stick. I calmed down for a while. When I resumed shaking, he hit me again. The sequence was repeated several times. Finally, he stopped, though I continued to shake throughout the remainder of the sitting.

This problem remained with me throughout my stay at

Chozen-Ji. Every evening, during the second evening sitting, no matter what I did, I would shake. I tried to control it by forcing my breath harder into my hara. Surprisingly, this often made the shaking worse. I knew the shaking was a reaction to the pain and I kept thinking that if only my body would relax, the sitting would not be painful and I would be able to stop shaking. Each night the jikijitsu would stand before me and help me try to regain control. He had the option to dismiss me from the sittings and I was concerned that I might be asked to leave the temple.

On the last night of my first stay at Chozen-Ji, I decided to keep from shaking no matter what it took. It would be the decisive battle; I wanted to leave the dojo with dignity. I took my position for the first sitting and steeled myself for the onslaught of pain. After about five minutes, I felt something drop onto my head and start moving. "It could only be a centipede!" I thought. Earlier in the day, while digging, we had unearthed a number of them. Because they are poisonous, we always gave them wide berths. Occasionally, they drop from the rafters onto the floor of the meditation hall below. While I had never heard of one landing on someone, there had to be a first time. I fought the urge to brush it off and resolved that I would get bitten before I would move. With sweat streaming down my face, I felt it crawl on my head for the next half hour, until the bell sounded ending the sitting. I did not get bitten and I did not move. I quietly exited the hall and brushed the creature off my head. To my surprise, it wasn't even a centipede, but a harmless black beetle. Laughing out loud on the verandah, I thought that if I could sit through that, I could sit through the second period without shaking.

I walked back into the meditation hall feeling more confident. I sat back down on my cushion. Somebody came up to me and bowed. I leaned forward and was told that Tanouye Roshi wanted to talk to me. I got up and went into the kitchen. Earlier in the day a visiting Japanese kyudo master, Onuma Sensei, had visited the dojo. The roshi told me that he had just had emergency surgery and asked me to accompany Mrs. Tanouye to the hospital to talk to the doctors. He wanted us to leave immediately. I missed the second round of zazen; the decisive battle was postponed.

Two years after leaving Chozen-Ji I returned for two weeks. In the interval, I had continued to practice zazen and felt that my sitting had improved. However, I had seldom sat for periods as long as the evening zazen at Chozen-Ji. I was anxious to see if I could make it through both sittings without shaking. During the second round of the first night, the familiar pains returned, and with them, the shaking. However, this time I was able to control them by concentrating on breathing slowly and deeply. This stopped the shaking and I never experienced it again. I also understood better what Tanouye Toshi had told me in Chicago about taking the pain up by my hara.

What had changed? Why was I able to control the shaking which had bothered me so much before? I had acquired better control of my breathing and posture in the intervening period. I realized that two years earlier I was tensing my upper torso, especially my chest and neck, in reaction to the pain. The muscular tension caused even more pain; which, in turn, resulted in more tension, causing me to shake. The shaking was an involuntary way of discharging the tension. The tension also made it difficult for me to breath properly. When I tried to set my hara, I also tensed the muscles in my upper body; this made the shaking worse. On that second visit to Chozen-Ji I realized I had learned to use my breath to relax the muscles in my upper torso rather than tightening them in the face of pain. I also understood better what Tanouye Roshi had told me in Chicago about taking the pain up by my hara. By being able, in the face of pain, to relax my upper body and tense my lower abdomen while maintaining deep abdominal breathing, I was able to detach myself from the pain.

My expectations of being able to sit without pain had also changed. I had thought it was possible to sit without pain and that there was something wrong with me because I could not. When I saw other students sitting, particularly those more advanced than I, I assumed they were not in as much pain as I. Even when they told me they found zazen painful or difficult, I did not quite believe them. Or, I assumed that because of my unusual lack of flexibility, the amount of pain I felt was much greater than theirs. However, the more I talked to other students, the more I came to believe them. I realized they sat better because they could tolerate pain better than I. This became clear to me when I saw students who were even stiffer than I sit, not only without shaking, but also without appearing to be in much pain. It finally became clear that my problem was not so much flexibility or the amount of pain that it caused; the problem was my intolerance of that pain. Instead of waiting for a miracle to happen that would enable me to sit painlessly, I realized I had to focus on learning to live with the pain.

Today I can sit for long periods of time without undue distress. I have been able to sit through sesshin without the difficulties that I experienced earlier on. In part, this is because the pain has decreased. But, as my breathing has improved, I have been able to relax my body even more. While my posture is certainly not equivalent to those more limber people able to sit full lotus from the beginning, it has improved substantially. I am also able to tolerate the pain better. I can detach myself from pain so that it does not distract me as it once did.

My difficulties with flexibility and posture are certainly not unique. Many Westerners, raised sitting in chairs rather than on the floor, have difficulty sitting cross-legged. Because of differences in anatomy, this appears to be truer for men than women. I know there are those who suggest that Westerners meditate in chairs or in the kneeling position if the cross-legged positions are uncomfortable. For me, this would have been a mistake. I feel strongly that I made the right decision when I arrived at Chozen-Ji. I am convinced the cross-legged positions are superior because, more so than kneeling and sitting in a chair, they promote proper breathing and posture. Fighting the pain caused by sitting cross-legged was an important growth experience for me. In a way my stiffness was an advantage. By having to fight the pain, I had no alternative but to improve my breath control in order to contain it.

In the last few years I have been teaching introductory workshops in zazen geared to people studying martial arts. Many of the participants have great difficulty sitting cross-legged and want to know about alternative positions. I try to discourage them from abandoning the half-lotus and lotus positions. In most cases I can honestly tell them I was stiffer than they when I began. I tell them that if I can sit cross-legged, then almost anybody can. Most of the time I feel that they do not believe me. I see them react as I did to Tanouye Roshi at that first sesshin. I also tell them that Zen training is difficult; that one way or another, they will have to overcome obstacles in themselves that can cause considerable pain and suffering.

For those students who have little difficulty with the physical aspects of training, there will be other inner obstacles to overcome in the course of training. Zen training is a constant struggle against the ego, which is the seat of thoughts and emotions that cloud our awareness. These thoughts and feelings, referred to collectively as delusions, are often compared to demons. They swarm over us and seduce us into pursuing them. Over the course of training, one becomes aware of how pervasive such delusions are and how difficult it is to break the grip they have over us.

Shortly after I started studying kyudo at Chozen-Ji, Tanouye Roshi asked me what I thought of it. I said something like, "It's very difficult." Tanouye Roshi said, "Yes, the target doesn't move." His comment underscored a very important principle in kyudo.

Written on the target house of the kyudo dojo at Chozen-Ji is the Japanese saying "Senshobutsu-Hankyushin." Jackson Morisawa translates it as "correcting things first runs counter to the search for oneself."[1] A more colloquial translation of this same saying is "When the gentleman archer misses his mark, he looks inward."

Because the target is stationary in kyudo, one must accept full responsibility for one's performance. Any imperfection of the shot comes from imperfection in oneself. In this sense, the target is internal. To cut through the waves of delusional thoughts that cloud our perception, to destroy the ego; that is the true target in kyudo. This is shown in an old poem:

> No target's erected
> No bow's drawn
> And the arrow leaves the string:
> It may not hit,
> But it does not miss.[2]

Carved over the entrance to the tea room which adjoins the kyudo dojo at Chozen-Ji is the Japanese saying "Mu-i," which means "fearlessness." The word alludes to a story told about Yamoaka Tesshu, a nineteenth-century lay Zen master, who was also a master of kendo and shodo. Omori Rotaishi is successor to Tesshu's lines of kendo and shodo. The story is as follows:

A young fencer who asked him about the inmost secret of the Way of fencing was told to go to the Kannon Temple at Asakusa and pray to be given enlightenment about it.

After a week the man came back and said, "I went every day and prayed for a long time but nothing came in response. But as I was coming away yesterday, for the first time I noticed what is written above the shrine: THE GIFT OF FEARLESSNESS. Was that what you meant?"

"It was," replied Tesshu. "The secret of our Way is complete fearlessness. But it has to be complete. Some there are who are not afraid to face enemies with swords, but who cringe before the assaults of passions like greed and delusions like fame. The end of our Way of fencing is to have no fear at all when confronting the inner enemies as well as the outer enemies."[3]

In kyudo, we must look inward and face our inner enemies. As one progresses in kyudo, one gains increasing insight into one's psychological makeup. This is a painful process, for we must acknowledge flaws in our character that make us miss our mark. Greed, competitiveness, vanity, self-criticism, shyness, fear, need for approval are but a few of the personality characteristics that can lead to delusive thoughts that cloud our awareness in kyudo. We must recognize these flaws before we can transcend them.

I started teaching kyudo about one year after returning to the United States. Shortly afterwards, I developed a problem with my release. For some reason, my arrows started flying wildly; at times they would even travel end over end. Although I was shooting from a distance of three feet, they would either miss the makiwara entirely or they would hit it at an angle and not penetrate. Either way, the arrows hit the dojo walls, leaving a series of holes in the plaster. I could not figure out why this was happening.

I became depressed over this and was embarrassed to let my students see such poor performance; what kind of role model would I be if I shot so poorly? I started to hide my problem from them by not shooting during class. Even practicing alone, I became increasingly self-conscious about my release. Eventually I stopped practicing altogether. I was 10,000 miles from my teachers in Hawaii and worried that by the time I saw Mr. Morisawa again, this bad habit would be so ingrained that it would be extremely difficult to break. I felt I was letting my teachers and students down.

In desperation, I went to Chicago to have another kyudo student see me shoot. He pointed out that I was flinching the instant before the release. Instead of increasing tension throughout kai by allowing the force of my breath steadily to expand my chest, I was losing control of my breath at the last moment. When I lost my hara, my chest contracted. Because my right elbow was not locked properly behind my shoulder, this contraction allowed my right hand to be pulled abruptly towards the bow, causing a jerky release and, in turn, the erratic flight of the arrow.

I went back to Madison and concentrated on my breathing and posture while shooting. This enabled me to maintain the continuous pressure necessary for the release. My arrows once again flew in a straight trajectory.

Once I had corrected my release, I realized there was a deeper significance to the problem I had been having: it reflected the insecurity I had about my new role as kyudo teacher. My desire to impress my students had "stopped my mind" and interrupted my breathing and posture. My flinching at the moment of truth came from fear that I would not shoot impressively. It was a way of cringing psychologically, and physically, at the prospect of failure. It perpetuated itself: the more I cringed, the worse I shot; the worse I shot, the more tentative I became. It was difficult for me to acknowledge that, at my stage of training, I still had such insecurity. However, once acknowledged, I was able to overcome it. I also realized that I had made a fundamental mistake by hiding my problems from my students. Had I been unafraid to shoot poorly in front of them, I would have been a much better model. By failing to look inward when I missed my mark, I also missed the opportunity to demonstrate an important principle of kyudo.

When Zen was introduced from China' to Japan in the thirteenth century, it was readily adopted by the samurai class in Kamakura. Some say they were attracted to it because it helped them overcome their fears of death.[4] Fear of death is attachment to life. Such attachment could distract them on the battlefield and decrease their effectiveness and ultimately speed their deaths. The samurai were known as great students of Zen. This has been attributed to the fact that for them Zen training was a life and death issue. The application of Zen principles to the fighting arts gave rise to the martial arts now referred to as Do or Ways. The practice of the arts became, at their highest levels, ways to cut through delusions, ways to fight the ego. Instruments that once were weapons of war become tools of self-development. The arrow in kyudo is aimed at oneself.

Chozen-Ji is a Zen temple in the tradition of the samurai in that it integrates Zen training with training in the Ways. However, few students today view their Zen or martial arts training with the urgency of the samurai. Nevertheless, the struggle of the Zen student today and that of the samurai is the same; it is a struggle with oneself, with one's ego. To impress students with the seriousness of Zen training and to motivate them to discipline themselves, attempts are made to foster in them the intensity of the samurai. At Chozen-Ji, it is common for students to be admonished for "losing" to dishes they were washing or the food they were eating. This is a way of saying that they allowed themselves to get distracted in the midst of an activity. A similar lapse of concentration in a critical situation, such as battle, could mean death.

In explaining the importance of the kyudo dojo, Jackson Morisawa writes:

> The Dojo is literally the battlefield of life, a "field of life and death." The only difference between it and the battlefield of war is that in the Dojo the trainee may die many times over and live to count these deaths as experiences which benefit his development in the ways and eventually to be able to transcend life and death."[5]

Here Mr. Morisawa is referring to the ongoing struggle with the ego. The student who approaches kyudo with the spirit that it is in fact a war—a war with oneself—will progress the most quickly. In this war, one must face physical and psychological pain in order to experience the fruits of victory.

The point of experiencing pain and suffering inside the dojo is to be able to face pain and suffering in everyday life. Zanshin is incomplete if mushin cannot be maintained in the face of adversity. In this vein, Tanouye Roshi once told me how business men often come to him for advice on business matters. He told me that in many instances his advice proved to be sound, resulting in considerable financial gain to his advisees.

When I heard this, I was surprised. He quickly cut off my reaction by saying, "Teaching people to make money is one thing. Helping them maintain their dignity while going bankrupt is another." He then went on to tell about times he had done just that—helped people maintain their dignity in the midst of bankruptcy. Another time he said that it is easy for people to be happy when they are happy. The challenge of Zen is to be happy when you are sad.

By learning to maintain equipoise whether one hits or misses the target in the kyudo dojo, one learns to maintain equipoise in daily life. The setbacks and frustrations in kyudo become a microcosm in which one learns to face the trials and tribulations of life. One learns to maintain proper breathing, posture, and concentration whether or not the arrow hits its mark so one can face difficulties in life in the same fashion. One learns to take up pain in one's hara in the dojo so that one can live with hara at all times.

The true test of a kyudoka's zanshin is his reaction to disappointments in life. It is insufficient for a kyudo student to maintain composure when he misses the target only to become unnerved by life's problems. Similarly, it is insufficient for him to look inward when he misses the paper target only to blame others for inadequacies that cause problems for him outside the dojo. The kyudo student endeavors to take life's difficulties in stride. To face hardships and disappointments with the calm that one has when one misses the target; to have the same composure in the face of calamity that the master has when his string breaks at full draw; to accept full responsibility for one's mistakes and to try again; that is true zanshin. The student who strives to live his life that way understands that the true target in kyudo is not the piece of paper that is ninety feet away; the true target is within.

CHAPTER 8

Kiai

"Your arrows do not carry," observed the Master,
"because they do not reach far enough spiritually."

Eugen Herrigel[1]

One day during my first stay at Chozen-Ji, I helped load a truck
with fallen timber to be hauled to the city dump. Afterwards, I
started up the driveway to the front of the temple grounds,
oblivious to the fact that the loaded truck was about to hit me.
Seeing this, Tanouye Roshi cuffed me on the shoulder to get me
out of the way. This, however, was no ordinary cuff. While I
felt his hand touch my shoulder, his touch was light. At the
same time, it was electrifying. There was a force behind him
that exceeded the combined mass and velocity of his hand. It
jolted me to attention and I jumped out of danger. Looking up,
I saw Tanouye Roshi looking at me and shaking his head in a
manner that, by then, had become quite familiar. It took me a
few minutes to figure out what had happened.

There is, in Eastern thought, a belief in a force the Japanese
call ki and the Chinese call ch'i. In short, ki can best be
described as the basic driving force of the Universe. It is the
universal energy from which all substance and all life is made.
It is also the driving force behind consciousness and, for that
reason, is often described as "psychophysical energy."

I first heard of ki at a martial arts demonstration when I was
in high school. I was told that, through the practice of the
martial arts, it is possible to learn to tap into that cosmic
energy and channel it in a way that produces a power different
from that of muscular strength. I learned that the names of two

major martial arts systems, tai ch'i and aikido, are, even in
name, based on the concept of ki. The former can be translated
as "great ch'i" and the other as the "Way of harmonizing with
ki." I also understood that the development of the powers of ki
was in some way linked to breathing. This was supposed to be
shown by something known as a ki-ai, which is a type of yell
that is supposed to come from the core of one's being.

I heard and read of such accounts of ki with ambivalence.
On the one hand, I found myself fascinated with the concept
and wanted to learn as much about it as possible; I wanted to
believe in it. On the other hand, I dismissed it as a sort of
fantasy, a kind of superstition that I equated with astrology or
reincarnation.

My skepticism about ki was bolstered when I began studying
martial arts some six years later. Remembering ki, I asked my
karate instructors what they thought of it. They debunked the
idea, explaining that the phenomena attributed to the force of
ki could be explained by the laws of physics. For example, they
referred to an aikido exercise called the "unbendable arm." In
this exercise, two people face each other while standing. One
person puts his forearm, with the elbow facing downward, on
the other's shoulder. The second person clasps both of his
hands on the first person's arm and exerts pressure so as to try
to force the first person to bend his arm at the elbow. If the first
person is able to do this exercise properly, he will be able to
resist having his elbow bent, without resorting to brute force. It
is not supposed to be a test of muscular strength.

The "metaphysical" explanation of the exercise suggests that
the first person, the one resisting, can direct the ki in his body
to flow through his arm so that the force of ki will be able to
keep his elbow from bending. The force of ki in this exercise is
often likened to water flowing through a hose. That ki is
operating in this exercise would be shown by the first person
resisting having his elbow bent without tensing the muscles of
his arm. However, my karate instructors convinced me that, if
the first person bent his arm at a very slight angle, it would put

the second person at a mechanical disadvantage making it difficult for him to bend the arm further. What some called ki, they convinced me, was actually explainable by the less esoteric laws of biomechanics. Gradually, I lost interest in the idea of ki.

When I was introduced to Zen by Mike Sayama, I was surprised to learn that he took the existence of ki as a given. I gathered that it played an important role in training at Chozen-Ji. When I first heard Tanouye Roshi lecture on Zen at the first sesshin I attended, he used the term closely related to ki, kiai. Kiai literally means "harmony with ki" and typically refers to a specific manifestation or embodiment of ki.[2] He told the following story:

> A wealthy man wanted to give a very large sum of money to a Zen temple. However, he explained that there was one stipulation: He asked to be able to observe the monks in zazen. This was a highly irregular request, since by protocol only the monks were allowed in the hall during zazen. But his financial offer was so generous that the abbot of the temple found it very difficult to turn down. So, they worked out a compromise of sorts. The patron was told that if he came to the temple at such and such a time he would be able to observe the monks from the outside through a knot hole in the wall. Before zazen began on the designated day, the abbot told the monks to sit as intensely as they could. And they did. When the patron arrived and put his eye to the knot hole, he was knocked over backwards by the kiai that was generated by the monks.

I politely listened to this story, as I did whenever he spoke about kiai. I guessed that Zen masters were not beyond superstitions.

About two years later, I was at a professional conference in Monterey, California. When it was over, I rented a car and drove to Tassajara where I spent a day and night. Tassajara is a training center of the San Francisco Zen Center and is the site of some well known hot springs. In the fall, winter, and spring, it is closed to the public. However, during the summer, it is transformed into a sort of resort where guests can stay and take part in scaled-down Zen training. I had been interested in seeing Tassajara for some time and was pleased they could accommodate me on short notice.

At the time, the person in charge of Tassajara was an American Zen Buddhist nun. I never spoke to her and only observed her from a distance. I noticed that when she looked directly at me, she had quite a sense about her. She had penetrating eyes which conveyed a sense of strength and calm. When she looked at me, I felt uncomfortable. Her stillness made me aware of my lack of stillness. Something about her calmness exerted some sort of power over me. I felt extremely self-conscious.

Whenever I walked past her, I stumbled. Sometimes I actually fell. This was true even if she was quite a distance from me. On several occasions I tripped and fell without seeing her; but, on getting up and looking around, I noticed that she was in the vicinity and was, in fact, looking at me. This all seemed quite odd to me. I thought of the story that Tanouye Roshi told about the patron being toppled over backwards when he saw the monks engaged in zazen. Maybe there was something to this idea of ki. Or maybe I was imagining things. Still, my stumbling happened with such regularity that it seemed unlikely that it was coincidental. A wedge began to be driven into my skepticism.

Any further skepticism that I might have had about ki was finally laid to rest by that tap on the shoulder by Tanouye Roshi. It was such a unique and shocking experience that I could not find another explanation for it. Somehow Tanouye Roshi was able to tap into a type of energy that I had never experienced. That tap on the shoulder was a "crack in the cosmic egg" for me. It changed my view of the world and of the Universe.

I have heard Tanouye Roshi say that when one becomes "one with mu," one becomes a conduit for ki. This emphasizes the psychophysical aspects of ki and kiai: mushin, the state of being "one with mu," is the state of proper harmony of breathing, posture, and concentration. This harmony of mind and body allows one to harmonize with the life force, ki. When one is in harmony with ki, one develops an inner power, power that can be experienced by other people. Kiai is often used to describe this inner strength; it is an inner strength that comes from stillness of the mind and body. To say that someone has strong kiai means that they convey this power. The term "spiritual energy" can also be used to describe kiai.

In explaining kiai, Tanouye Roshi often emphasizes the role of breathing. He maintains that when one is breathing properly (which depends on one's posture and concentration), one actually changes the quality of one's vibrations. In the process, one becomes in greater harmony with ki. The seat of this vibration is the tanden, the center of the hara, which is the center of one's being. Zen breathing, whether in zazen or in the Zen arts, changes one's rate of vibration by focusing on the tanden. This, then, creates the state of mind associated with mushin.

Tanouye Roshi often uses musical analogies when explaining how breathing affects the body's vibrations. It takes a music student many years to perfect the tone he can produce on a musical instrument. For example, a novice flute player will make an unpleasant sound. With practice, he can make a mellower tone. If he goes on to become a virtuoso, he will produce outstanding notes with the same flute. The difference between the novice, intermediate and virtuoso player is the dynamics of his breath. With increasing skill, his breath changes the way the flute vibrates, creating ever more pleasing sounds.

Tanouye Roshi likens the Zen student to the musician. When he begins the practice of zazen, the quality of his breath is poor and the body's vibrates like the novice's flute. This is reflected in an inability to concentrate. With further practice, the Zen student gains control over his breath. As he slows and deepens his respirations, the vibrations in his body become mellower and he is able to concentrate better. At some point in his practice, a psychophysical shift will occur; his breathing will produce the proper vibrations at the tanden and he will enter mushin.

As another illustration of how breathing can influence the rate at which one vibrates and how this, in turn, can influence one's state of mind, Tanouye Roshi refers to the practicing of chanting in Zen. It is traditional for Zen trainees to chant certain Buddhist texts and passages as part of their training. Usually this is done in a large group, with one person leading the chants and others keeping cadence with a drum and gongs. Some of the passages that are chanted are in Chinese or Japanese. Tanouye Roshi feels that these should be chanted in the original languages, rather than chanting the English translations of them. The sound of the words and the rhythm of the cadence cause vibrations which establish mushin. This is more important than understanding the words that are chanted. Chanting English translations of these passages changes the qualities of the sounds and rhythm that are so powerful.

Other chants involve the recitation of nonsense syllables. Again, the sounds and rhythms of the chants establish the proper frame of mind. According to Tanouye Roshi, by forming the sounds through deep, abdominal breaths, the vibrations emanate from the tanden. These vibrations are so compelling they can influence the people around them; they can put people into mushin. Tanouye Roshi also explains that when a whole group of chanters are chanting properly, their vibrations interact sympathetically so as to boost the level of kiai of the whole group.

My initial reaction to such explanations of chanting was disbelief. I was willing to view chanting as good breath control exercise, but the idea of vibrations seemed too esoteric for me. Then, I had some experiences which made me give up my skepticism.

One afternoon at Suhara Osho's dojo in Japan, he called out my name and motioned for me to follow him. He led me to the old main gate of the temple. I had long been curious about this gate. It is a sort of elevated housing, and is a well known feature of Engaku-Ji. For a long time it had been open to the public. However, it was eventually closed off to prevent wear and tear on the old structure.

To my surprise, Suhara Osho led me up the stairs and into the gate itself. There I saw a gathering of priests; there must have been twenty to thirty of them. Suhara Osho introduced me to one who spoke flawless English. He explained to me that the gate is opened once a year, for the Engaku-Ji priests only. He told me that they had gathered in order to chant. He showed me around the interior, pointing out many of the Buddhist icons that were along the wall. Finally, he told me that I would now have to leave because the priests were going to start chanting. I thanked both him and Suhara Osho and left the building alone.

As I started down the path leading back to the kyudo dojo, I heard a gong followed by the sound of priests chanting. But I did not just hear the chanting, I actually felt it with a visceral intensity. It was similar to sitting next to a loud pipe organ that is playing bass. However, the chanting was not loud. The sound and the vibrations had a compelling, penetrating quality. It reached inside me. I started to feel calm and serene. My breathing became deeper and slower. I sat down on the ground and listened until the chanting ended. When I saw the priests leave the gate, I went back and practiced kyudo. The sense of calm remained with me for some time.

Another formative experience occurred at a sesshin in Chicago several years ago. Over the course of a sesshin the kiai grows. As the participants refine their breathing, posture and concentration over long periods of zazen, the group acquires a collective sense of harmony. The body relaxes; the breath becomes deeper and slower; the senses sharpen. This particular sesshin had been especially intense for me, and by the end of sesshin I felt that my breathing had changed substantially. One of the last activities of the sesshin was chanting. As I began to chant, I noticed that it did in fact feel as if the sounds that I was making were coming out of my lower abdomen. Then, it felt like the inside of my lower abdomen was vibrating. These vibrations felt as if they were radiating into the room. Simultaneously, I felt vibrations coming from the other chanters. Their vibrations and mine were in synchrony. It was as if we were all vibrating sympathetically. A sense of tranquility and clarity came over me as I felt in harmony with the others.

Just as the vibrations caused by chanting can influence another person's state of mind, so too can one be affected while in the presence of someone in harmony with the Universal flow. Mushin can be transferred by association, so to speak. I first realized this when I saw a sharei, which is a formal kyudo ceremony. It was at the end of my stay at Chozen-Ji that Onuma Sensei, the kyudo master from Japan, paid a visit to the temple. As part of his visit, he performed a sharei. As I watched him go through the slow, deliberate movements of the ceremony, I started to feel increasingly at peace. Everything around me appeared crystal clear; I felt as if I could see 180 degrees. My breathing became slower and deeper. My breaths adopted the rhythm of his. I was picking up on Onuma Sensei's state of mind; in other words, I was picking up on his kiai.

One of Tanouye Roshi's first Zen students was a Catholic nun named Sister Ruth. I first met her in 1984 when she spent six weeks in Madison training to become a hospital chaplain. One day she related to me an incident that had recently happened. She had been called in to see a woman with terminal cancer. This woman was in agony and told Sister Ruth she was afraid to die. As she related the story, Sister Ruth stayed with her for about another hour and finally the woman said to her, "You may go now, I don't need you any more." Sister Ruth went back to visit the woman over the next two days but, as Sister Ruth put it, she had already "crossed over" and did not acknowledge her presence. However, she did appear at peace. Finally the woman died.

As I understand what went on between Sister Ruth and this woman, Sister Ruth transferred her own state of mind to the woman. I am convinced that Sister Ruth has no fear of death. While I might have been able to tell the woman that there is nothing to fear, or that I am not afraid to die, it would not have had the same power because it would not have been true. My insincerity and, behind that, my own fear of death would have been apparent. But with Sister Ruth, words were not important. Her inner peace in the face of death was transferred to the woman. This could have been conveyed by almost anything she said. I feel this way because of my reaction when Sister Ruth related the incident. I could sense that she truly did not fear death. I could feel the inner strength born of stillness coming from her.

The person with strong kiai does not always have a pleasant or calming effect. The inner strength born of stillness can penetrate and make more people aware of their own restlessness. That was my experience at Tassajara. I also do not want to imply that being around a Zen master is always pleasant. Because of their developed kiai, their comments can have tremendous intensity that can cut to the quick. During sesshin even advanced students are sometimes so intimidated by the prospect of meeting the master during sanzen that they refuse to go voluntarily and have to be carried bodily out of the meditation hall.

As I mentioned earlier, in martial arts there is a type of yell that is referred to as a ki-ai. What I learned a long time ago is true. When done properly, it is not an ordinary yell. The proper ki-ai (yell) should come from deep within the hara and should produce vibrations like those generated in chanting. It is a vocal projection of energy. Such a ki-ai is a unification of breathing, posture, and concentration that focuses the power of a move. Actually, this focusing of power is a channeling of ki.

At Chozen-Ji, we sometimes make a ki-ai when releasing the

arrow. The force of the breath necessary to make a loud ki-ai emphasizes the force of breath necessary for a proper release. If the kyudoka's breathing, posture and concentration are not in harmony, the force of the ki-ai will be experienced as jolt which will interfere with the release of the arrow. However, if proper unity of body and mind has been reached, the force of the ki-ai will be chaneled smoothly into the release of the arrow. The vocal ki-ai, then, is an expression of the kyudoka's level of spiritual energy.

Several years ago I showed Suhara Osho some photographs a student of mine had taken of him as he performed a sharei at a demonstration in Belgium as part of the cultural exchange during which he met Tanouye Roshi. We went through the sequence of photographs, which showed him at the various stages of hassetsu. When we came to the shot taken immediately after the release, Suhara Osho noticed that the picture was blurred. He laughed and explained that he made a loud ki-ai on the release of the arrow. This must have jolted the photographer, he said, resulting in a blurred image.

In *Zen in the Art of Archery*, Eugen Herrigel describes how, when he first started to shoot at the mato, as opposed to the makiwara (practice target), his arrow did not even travel the ninety-foot distance. The following explanation and instructions were given to him by his master:

"Your arrows do not carry," observed the Master, "because they do not reach far enough spiritually. You must act as if the goal were infinitely far off. For master archers it is a fact of common experience that a good archer can shoot further with a medium-strong bow than an unspiritual archer can with the strongest. It does not depend on the bow, but on the presence of mind, on the vitality and awareness with which you shoot. In order to unleash the full force of this spiritual awareness you must perform the ceremony differently: rather as a good dancer dances. If you do this, your movements will spring from the center, from the seat of right breathing. . . . By performing the ceremony like a religious dance, your spiritual awareness will develop its full force."[3]

The "force of spiritual awareness" that Master Awa spoke of is kiai. At the point of release, there should be a sense of unity between one's breathing, posture, and concentration. Without this, the shot would not be "spiritual" as Master Awa would say. The feeling should be that the arrow is propelled simultaneously by the force of one breath and by one's awareness, which does not stop at the target but extends past the target into infinity. This can only be accomplished if the release is natural, and the release can only be natural if body and mind are unified. When the perfect cross is reached, one harmonizes with the life flow of the Universe and channels it into the act of shooting an arrow. Master Awa's advice to Herrigel on how to perform the ceremony actually reinforces the importance of breathing, posture, and concentration. To do the "dance" properly, one must establish proper breathing, posture, and concentration. This sets the stage for the proper state of body and mind at the point of the release of the arrow. It enables the kyudoka to start building kiai before the release.

Of course, the idea in kyudo is not just to develop kiai when one is shooting an arrow. One trains in kyudo in order to experience it in daily life. The person with kiai conveys that power of stillness in everything that he does. The person with kiai lives the principles of kyudo in daily life. And the person who lives the principles of kyudo harmonizes with life; that is, he has spiritual energy called kiai.

I am convinced the jolt that I experienced that day when Tanouye Roshi tapped me on the shoulder is best explained as kiai; the channeling of psychophysical energy, ki, through him. It was as much an expression of that energy as that which I feel in sanzen or while chanting. I certainly do not understand how he did it. However, that event made me realize that what I had read as a teenager was true: in the martial arts it is possible to channel a power that is above and beyond that of muscular strength. Nor is this power limited to practitioners of the martial arts; it is a by-product of training in Zen and the Ways. Many stories like the following are told:

> Daito Kokushi, a great Japanese Rinzai Master, lived among beggars to refine himself by living under the worst possible conditions. Once a degraded samurai came to test a new sword on a beggar. Daito told the others to hide and sat in meditation. The samurai approached Daito, drew his sword, and said, "Get ready. My sword is going to cut you in two." Daito did not move. An awe came over the samurai who hesitated and beat a retreat.[4]

I do not mean to imply that spiritual energy belongs only to the province of Zen. Many of the great religious leaders have the qualities that can be described as kiai. Zen and the Ways provide one method for training people in those qualities. So, too, are there charismatic people in many walks of life who have a personal power that can be compared to kiai. However Zen and the Ways provide structured training methods designed to develop kiai. As such, they have few, if any, counterparts in the West.

CHAPTER 9
The Journey West

The bow is the rainbow.

Suhara Koun Osho

On a hot August day I went to say goodbye to Suhara Osho. My time in Japan had come to an end; I was leaving the next day for the United States. We shot a few rounds of arrows together, then drank tea in silence. He escorted me to the main gate, stepped outside, and stopped. We bowed, then shook hands. He remained on the top step while I walked down to the train station. When I was half way down, he called out "Kushner-San!" I turned around and saw him mimic the draw and release of an arrow. I laughed, then bowed. I understood what he was telling me: "Keep on practicing!" I turned and continued down the steps, turned around again, and saw him waving at me. He continued to wave until I disappeared from sight. The Japanese call the ritual of sending someone off zanshin; the same word as the last stage in the shooting sequence.

On the plane ride home, I reflected on how fortunate I had been in my journey to Hawaii and Japan. While abroad, I met many Westerners who had gone there looking for a spiritual experience like that described by Herrigel in *Zen in the Art of Archery*. However, because Japanese tradition makes it difficult to study with a teacher without a formal introduction, few were able to find what they were looking for.

The next time I returned to Chozen-Ji was two and a half years later. In front of the entrance to the kyudo dojo I saw a stone monument which had not been there before. Etched on the stone is a picture of a rainbow. Next to that are Japanese characters that read "Yumi wa niji nari" ("The bow is the rainbow"). This saying comes from an experience that Suhara Osho had during his first visit to Chozen-Ji. In his words:

I had never thought of the rainbow in Japan. But when I came to Chozen-Ji, through the introduction of Tanouye Roshi, I saw a very beautiful rainbow after a rain shower. In Japan we usually see only a partial rainbow. But in Hawaii, the rainbow stretched from mountain to mountain and had very clear and deep colors and was shining. I went out of the building and was making gassho when I came to myself. At that time the phrase "a bow is a rainbow" flashed across my mind. It just came at that moment. A seven colored halo was shining just like the halo of Buddha. We have to draw a bow so that our personality can shine in seven colors. People should not be satisfied with hitting the target which is twenty-eight meters away. We have to split our spirit with an arrow and sincerely send it straight to the target. This is spiritual kyudo. Since then I have kept this phrase "the bow is a rainbow" in my mind. We have to be always humble in our daily life. This phrase implies that just consistently hitting the target is not the kyudo that I pursue. Even if an arrow doesn't hit the target, kyudo can be beautiful and good.[1]

The rainbow also symbolizes the transmission of "spiritual kyudo" from Japan to the West. Zen originated in India; it then spread to China and later Japan. Zen is now taking root in the West. So, too, is kyudo. Some day Westerners will not have to travel as far as I did to study the Way of the Bow. It is the hope of those at Chozen-Ji that the spirit of kyudo will spread from horizon to horizon, like a rainbow, uniting East and West for the good of all.

Notes

INTRODUCTION: ENTERING THE WAY

1 E. Herrigel, *Zen in the Art of Archery*, New York, Pantheon, 1971, p.3.
2 Due to the large number of Japanese terms used in the text, I have dispensed with the usual practice of italicizing foreign words. For the reader's convenience, a glossary is included at the end of the book. When using Japanese titles, I will follow the convention of placing the title after the person's name.
   In 1987 Hosokawa Dogen Roshi became the abbot of Chozen-Ji. Tanouye Tenshin Roshi became the Kancho (archbishop) of Daihonzan (main temple headquarters) Chozen-Ji. His proper title is now Tanouye Tenshin Rotaishi. However, since most of the incidents described in this book took place before this change, I will refer to him throughout as Tanouye Roshi in order to avoid confusion.
3 T. Leggett, *Zen and the Ways*, Boulder, Shambhala, 1978, p.117.
4 J. Morisawa, *Zen Kyudo*, Honolulu, International Zen Dojo, 1984.
5 M. Sayama, *Samadhi: Self Development in Zen, Swordsmanship, and Psychotherapy*, Ithaca, SUNY Press, 1986.

CHAPTER 1 TECHNIQUES AND PRINCIPLES

1 J. Morisawa, *Zen Kyudo*, Honolulu, International Zen Dojo, 1984, p.8.
2 T. Leggett, *Zen and the Ways*, Boulder, Shambhala, 1978, p.125.
3 A. Sollier and Z. Gyorbiro, *Japanese Archery, Zen in Action*, New York, Weatherhill, 1969, pp.75–6.
4 I will use the term "kyudoka" to refer to a practitioner of kyudo. It is tempting to use instead the less awkward English word, archer. However, the word archer does not have the spiritual connotations

of kyudoka (a person who follows a Way), just as Western archery must not be equated with kyudo.

5   T. Leggett, op. cit., p.125.

CHAPTER 2 BREATHING, POSTURE, AND CONCENTRATION

1   In this brief discussion of the connotations of the word hara, I have borrowed from Karlfried Graf Von Durckheim in his book, *Hara: The Vital Centre of Man* (London, Allen & Unwin, 1977). Readers intersted in learning more about the interconnections between the physical, psychologial and spiritual aspects of hara are referred to that book.

2   K. Von Durkheim, op. cit., p.31.

CHAPTER 3 MUSHIN

1   J. Morisawa, *Zen Kyudo*, Honolulu, International Zen Dojo, 1984, p.8.

2   D. T. Suzuki, *Zen and Japanese Culture*, Princeton, Princeton University Press, 1959.

3   P. Reps, *Zen Flesh, Zen Bones*, Garden City, Anchor, p.18.

4   E. Herrigel, *Zen in the Art of Archery*, New York, Pantheon, 1971, p.41.

5   D. T. Suzuki, op. cit., p.94.

CHAPTER 4 KOAN ZEN

1   J. Morisawa, *Zen Kyudo*, Honolulu, International Zen Dojo, 1984, 12.

2   Z. Shibayama, *Zen Comments on the Mumonkan*, New York, Harper & Row, 1974, p.12.

3   J. K. Kadowaki, *Zen and the Bible*, London, Routledge & Kegan Paul, 1980, p.73.

4   J. K. Kadowaki, op. cit.

5   Z. Shibayama, op. cit., p.286.

6   Z. Shibayama, op. cit., p.306.

7   E. Herrigel, *Zen in the Art of Archery*, New York, Pantheon, 1971, p.32.

8   J. Morisawa, op. cit., p.33.

CHAPTER 5 THE NATURALLY CORRECT WAY

1 D. T. Suzuki, *Training of the Zen Buddhist Monk*, New York, University Books, 1965, p.33.
2 T. Leggett, *Zen and the Ways*, Boulder, Shambhala, 1978, p.122.
3 J. Haley, *Uncommon Therapy: The Psychiatric Techniques of Milton Erickson*, New York, Norton, 1973, p.11. For a further treatment of Milton Erickson and his relationship to Zen see M. Sayama, *Samadhi: Self Development in Zen, Swordsmanship and Psychotherapy*, Ithaca, SUNY Press, 1986.
4 T. Leggett, *Encounters in Yoga and Zen: Meetings of Cloth and Stone*, London, Routledge & Kegan Paul, 1982, pp.25–6.
5 A. Sollier and Z. Gyorbiro, *Japanese Archery: Zen in Action*, New York, Weatherhill, 1969, pp.75–6.

CHAPTER 6 ZANSHIN

1 E. Herrigel, *Zen in the Art of Archery*, New York, Pantheon, 1971, p.60.
2 J. Morisawa, *Zen Kyudo*, Honolulu, International Zen Dojo, 1984, p.11.
3 D. T. Suzuki, *Zen and Japanese Culture*, Princeton University press, 1959, pp.117–19.

CHAPTER 7 PAIN

1 J. Morisawa, *Zen Kyudo*, Honolulu, International Zen Dojo, 1984, p.11.
2 D. T. Suzuki, *Zen and Japanese Culture*, Bollingen Series LXIV, copyright © by Princeton University Press, 1959, p.120. Reprinted with permission of Princeton University Press.
3 M. Sayama, *Samadhi: Self Development in Zen, Swordsmanship, and Psychotherapy*, Ithaca, SUNY Press, 1986, p.98.
4 T. Leggett, *Zen and the Ways*, Boulder, Shambhala, 1978, p.117.
5 J. Morisawa, op. cit., p.91.

CHAPTER 8 KIAI

1 E. Herrigel, *Zen in the Art of Archery*, New York, Pantheon, 1971, p.62.

2   In order to avoid confusion, the spelling ki-ai will be used when refering to the "yell" whereas kiai will be used when an a more general manifestation of ki. The Japanese character is the same in both instances, as is the pronunciation.

3   E. Herrigel, op. cit.

4   Quoted from the brochure of Chozen-Ji.

CHAPTER 9 THE JOURNEY WEST

1   The Japanese word for the bow used in archery, yumi, and the word for rainbow, niji, are not related as are their English counterparts. Therefore, the connection between the bow and the rainbow is not linguistically apparent in Japanese.

Glossary

Aikido The Way of harmony with *ki*; one of the martial Ways.

Ashibumi (to step or tread) First stage of *hassetsu*; to form a base stance.

Chado The Way of tea; tea ceremony.

Ch'i Chinese pronunciation of character pronounced *ki* in Japanese.

Daisan (the great third) Intermediate step in the stage of *hikiwake* in which the bow is one third drawn.

Do (Way) A path towards spiritual enlightenment; a Zen art.

Dojo (Place of the Way) Place where *Do* is practiced; training hall.

Dozukuri (Setting the torso in place) Second stage of *hassetsu*; to form a strong base.

Gassho Pressing the palms together in front of the body; a gesture of thanksgiving.

Hanare (To release) Seventh stage of *hassetsu*.

Hara The lower abdomen; fortitude of character.

Hassetsu The eight stages of kyudo; the formalized shooting sequence.

Hikiwake (To draw the bow—drawing apart) Fifth stage of *hassetsu*.

Ji Techniques, in contrast to *ri*, principles; specific expression of *ri*.

Jikijitsu Person in charge of zazen in Zen temple or Zen dojo.

Kai (Meeting) Sixth stage of *hassetsu*; stage when all of the elements necessary to form the perfect cross come together.

Karate-do Way of the empty fist.

Kendo The Way of the sword; swordsmanship.

Ki Vital energy; the driving force of the universe.

Kiai (Harmony with ki) Embodiment of *ki*; spiritual energy.

Ki-ai A verbal expression of one's spiritual energy.

Koan A question, unsolvable by the rational mind, given to a student by a Zen master; both a way of testing a student's Zen understanding and of guiding him towards Zen understanding.

Kyudo Way of the bow.

Kyudoka Practitioner of kyudo.

Makiwara   Training target made of straw.

Mato   Target (shot at from a distance of ninety feet).

Mu   Empty, null or void.

Muri   Not in accord with *ri*; against reason.

Mushin   (Void heart/mind)   A state of integration of mind and body in which the mind is free from delusions (unnecessary thought).

Myo   Wondrous workings of the Universe.

Osho   Zen priest (title).

Ri   Underlying principles of the Universe; reason.

Rinzai   Sect of Zen known for its use of koans.

Roshi   (Venerable teacher)   Title reserved for heads of temples and older Zen masters.

Rotaishi   Old great master (title).

Samadhi   State of intense concentration where delusion is transcended; closely related to *mushin*.

Sanzen   Ritual in which student presents solution of *koan* to master.

Seiza   Position of sitting on knees with feet tucked under buttocks.

Sensei   Teacher (title).

Sesshin   (Settling of the spirit)   Intensive Zen training session, lasting several days to one week.

Sharei   Ceremonial form of kyudo.

Shodo   The Way of writing with a brush; "spiritual" calligraphy.

Susoku   Exercise of counting the breaths during *zazen*.

Tai Ch'i   (Great *ch'i*)   Chinese martial art

Tanden   Point approximately two inches below the navel; person's physical and spiritual center.

Tao   Chinese pronunciation of character pronounced *Do* in Japanese.

Uchiokoshi   (Lifting the bow)   Fourth stage of *hassetsu*.

Yugamae   (Setting the bow in place)   Third stage of *hassetsu*.

Zanshin   (Remaining heart/mind)   Eighth stage of *hassetsu*; continuity of spirit.

Zazen   (Sitting Zen)   Zen meditation.